Full Speed Ahead

The Story Behind the Founding of the Town of Farragut, Tennessee

by Heather Mays

FULL SPEED AHEAD

The Story Behind the Founding of the Town of Farragut, Tennessee

©2013 Farragut Community Group

Contact the publisher by visiting:

FullSpeedAheadBook.com

International Standard Book Number (ISBN): 978-0-9911905-0-8

Printed in the United States of America

First Printing: November 2013

CREDITS:

Charlie Daniel, cartoonist for the Knoxville News Sentinel, produced a number of cartoons related to the struggle to incorporate Farragut. We are indebted to Charlie for allowing us to use the cartoons in the book. They serve as a great backdrop for the narrative of the book.

Cover photo, graphic design and layout by Andy Roberts, www.Lumino-City.com

Contents Page

*"Whenever I have been in a difficult situation
or in the midst of such a confusion of details
that the simple and right thing to do seemed hazy,
I have often asked myself, '
What would Farragut do?'"*

ADMIRAL GEORGE DEWEY,
WHO DEDICATED A MONUMENT
TO THE U.S. NAVY'S FIRST ADMIRAL,
DAVID GLASGOW FARRAGUT,
AT A SITE NEAR THE TOWN OF FARRAGUT

Foreword

"When in the Course of human events, it becomes necessary for one people to dissolve the political bands which have connected them with another, and to assume among the powers of the earth, the separate and equal station to which the Laws of Nature and of Nature's God entitle them, a decent respect to the opinions of mankind requires that they should declare the causes which impel them to the separation."

Familiar words, right? They formed the first sentence of the Declaration of Independence, a document that set into motion a movement in which citizens took matters into their own hands to throw off an oppressive government and to form a new government. This document was the crucible of the American story, a story of sacrifice, courage, and honor. We all know the story well, and as long as remember and cherish that story, hope will never die in America.

The story of the founding of the Town of Farragut is just the story of America, repeated on a smaller scale. This book chronicles the journey of a small group of courageous people who managed to bring about the founding of the Town of Farragut against all odds.

The reader will get to know those people and the struggles they faced in this effort. They were ordinary people with a vision and a passion, while being quite diverse in experiences.

Admiral Farragut, himself, said it best when facing a particular formidable task; "Damn the torpedoes, full-speed ahead!" A fitting motto for a group 100+ years later as well as now and into the future.

We owe a great debt to Mrs. Heather Beck, the author. She was successful in portraying this group of people as real people with real lives and in making the book something more than a typical history book.

Preface

The idea of "Full Speed Ahead" wasn't mine.

In fact, I'm fairly certain that when Mayor Ralph McGill asked me if I'd be interested in writing a history of the 1980 founding of Farragut, he expected me to say no.

But I did say yes, and so began an 18-month process of interviews, lunches, meetings and writing to turn the recollections of a few dozen people into a cohesive story, one that accurately reflected history but centered on personalities.

And these personalities are what shape "Full Speed Ahead."

The book is a novelized telling of Farragut's foundation, divided into chapters depicting the historical actions of Knox County, the City of Knoxville and the citizens of the town that would become Farragut, and chapters introducing a few of the major personalities involved: people like Ralph McGill, Eric Johnson, Betty Dick, Ron Simandl, Gene McNalley, George Dorsey and David Rodgers.

These men's and women's personalities shaped the town Farragut became.

For the seven founders of Farragut, 1980 was about their personal fights and their personal victories as much as it was about the creation of a town. It was Ralph McGill's issues with stormwater, Ron Simandl's with sign clutter and Eric Johnson's with sight distances on roads that led to Farragut's eventual adoption of some of the strictest development rules in East Tennessee.

In this book you'll learn more than the strict historical tale of how Farragut incorporated and who was involved.

Hopefully, you will come to understand how the people who created Farragut also, through the sheer force of their personalities, shaped what the town has become and still shape it today.

~

A few notes:

Every person involved in the founding of Farragut is not mentioned or interviewed in the book — they simply could not be, for both space and time constraints. Hundreds of citizens, elected officials and government employees were involved in Farragut's incorporation from many sides, and their contributions are noted by history. "Full Speed Ahead" focuses on a few of the strongest personalities who shaped the 1980 fight over Farragut's incorporation. Any omission was done without prejudice.

This book was, regrettably, written without the direct memories of David Rodgers and Jess Campbell, both of whom passed away before "Full Speed Ahead" was begun. Many thanks go to their families and friends who helped fill in the spaces.

Thank you, also, to every person I interviewed for sharing his or her memories, stories, photographs and artwork. And for introducing me to those John Wayne movies.

Thank you for reading.

— Heather Mays

In 1980, "Airplane" was the number one movie in America. Mt. St. Helens erupted. CNN was launched. Czeslaw Milosz won the Nobel Prize for Literature.

1980 was a leap year and an election year. The 1980 Winter Olympics were held in Lake Placid, New York. The U.S. boycotted the Summer Olympics, which were held in Moscow. "The Empire Strikes Back" was released in May.

A massive heat wave hit the nation. In the World Series, the Philadelphia Phillies beat the Kansas City Royals 4-2 in game six. Iron Maiden released its debut album of the same name.

Ronald Reagan was elected president, defeating incumbent Jimmy Carter.

A record number of viewers tuned in to the season finale of TV soap opera "Dallas," to learn lead character J.R. Ewing had been shot. "Who shot J.R.?" became an international catchphrase. Robert DeNiro and Sissy Spacek won Academy Awards.

John Lennon, former Beatle, was assassinated in New York City.

In East Tennessee, Knox County government was restructured under a home rule charter, which went into effect in September 1980.

And in that county, a rag-tag group of engineers, attorneys, chemists, a nurse, a highway patrolmen and other professionals were starting a new town, one of the last to be incorporated in the state.

FARRAGUT COMMUNITY GROUP

Ralph and Marianne McGill
Jeremy and Elizabeth "Betty" Dick
Ron and Wanda Simandl
George and Julie Dorsey
David and Martha Ann "Marty" Rodgers
Clifton "Gene" and Eva McNalley
Eric and Jan Johnson
Jess Campbell
Tom Slawson
William "Bill" and Karen Etter
Dewey Young
Bill Sonnenthal
Lacey Harville

CONCERNED CITIZENS COMMITTEE

Larry Vaughan
Bill and Anne Shipley
Buddy White
Sam and Grace Guinn
Virginia Jones

FARRAGUT GOVERNMENT

Robert "Bob" Leonard—*Farragut Mayor, 1980 to 1993*

Farragut's first Board of Mayor and Aldermen, elected in 1980:
Bob Leonard, Marianne McGill, W. Edward "Eddy" Ford III,
George Dorsey, Eric Johnson

Municipal Planning Commission, 1981: Bob Leonard,
Marianne McGill, Michael Carle, Tom McFee, Tom Slawson,
Jeff Klopatek, Charles McMurray, Connie Rutenber and Larry Patrick

Board of Mayor and Alderman, 1981-1983: Mayor Bob Leonard,
Marianne McGill, Betty Dick, W. Edward "Eddy" Ford III, Ron Simandl

KNOXVILLE GOVERNMENT

Randy Tyree—*Knoxville Mayor, 1976 to 1983*
John Roach—*Knoxville Law Director*
Knoxville City Council members in 1980: M. T. Bellah,
Arthur Blanchard, Casey C. Jones, Joe T. Mitchell,
Mrs. Bernice M. O'Connor, Milton E. Roberts, Jack C. Sharp,
Jean Teague, W. Howard Temple

KNOX COUNTY GOVERNMENT

Judge C. Howard Bozeman

Knox County Quarterly Court in 1979: Walter Hardy, Billy Tindell,
William Schaad, Bee DeSelm, Ted Lundy, Robert Hill, Joseph Pennell,
Mary Lou Horner, Willard Yarbrough, Robert Easley, Jesse Cawood,
William Jones, Billy Walker, Joe McMillan, John Mills, Charles Drew,
Max Wolf, H.B. Jenkins and Olen Ford

Knox County Board of Commissioners: chairman Billy Tindell,
vice-chair Bill Detherage and secretary Jim McBee

Knox County Metropolitan Planning Commissioners: Harold Beal,
Mrs. Tom Stone, Edward H. Green, Wanda L. Moody,
Charles "Pete" Drew, Bee DeSelm, John Mann, Freddie R. Brasfield,
Walter H. McKelvey, Dr. E.E. Overton, James Spencer, John H.
Coleman, James E. Polhemus, Rev. Byron Ragsdale and Frank Leuthold

Knox County Election Commissioners in 1980: chair H. Gene Bell,
Richard Krieg, Edna Smyre, Gordon Baer, Bill Owen

FARRAGUT AREA SUBDIVISIONS

Village Green, Fox Den, Linda Heights, Kingsgate, Concord Hills,
Belleaire, Thornton Heights, Woodchase, Sweetbriar, Woodland Trace

The auditorium buzzed at the name.

Cas Walker was a bit of a legend in Knoxville—he'd had a radio variety show in the '20s that later became a television show. He had launched the career of the voluptuous Appalachian musician Dolly Parton.

Cas, the flamboyant politician, had been famously photographed punching a fellow Knoxville city councilman in the 1950s. He'd retired from politics in '71, but had remained active, working now to eliminate the possibility of a unified county and city government.

These days, he mostly ran his chain of grocery stores.

He was a multi-millionaire who still fit in better with the working class.

And now here he was, walking down the aisle of Farragut High School's auditorium after Jess Campbell had recognized him from the lectern and called him up.

God only knew what he was going to say.

Cas owned a few businesses nearby, and might very well be in opposition to the idea of incorporating this little town that would be called Farragut, and now Jess had called him up to speak, in front of those hundreds of people.

And even the Yankees in the room knew Cas had never had a case of stage fright.

He shuffled up the steps and walked down the stage to the microphone, cleared his throat and threw out a sly smile.

"You know ... you know, everyone wants to get to heaven," he began.

"But no one wants to die to get there."

PART I
The Revolution

The Idea

May 1979

She let out her breath with a *whoosh*.

They were big words that had just been uttered. The kinds of words you could come to remember fondly, with pride. Or with regret.

But they certainly weren't words anyone would say glibly.

The room was a little too quiet after the raucous complaining that had been going on—heated words over developers and crooked politicians, about roads riddled with potholes and floodways with houses being built in them. And a little talk about annexation ... about this moment being only the beginning of a lot more worries.

And now that Jess had said *those words*, everyone was quiet.

"We should just incorporate," he had said, slapping the coffee table in George and Julie Dorsey's living room for emphasis.

The idea had been bandied about before. Julie and Jess had in fact been working on incorporation plans for years as they served together on the Fox Den homeowners' association board. But the plans had never gone further than rudimentary research—Jess ran a busy law practice in downtown Knoxville and Julie worked as a chemist in Oak Ridge and had a family to care for. They might be fed up with the local government corruption, but they both had personal lives that had always ranked higher.

But a person could only put up with so much.

Jess's words reverberated around the room. They were the result of months of frustration, finally pouring out over bottles of beer and shared stories of governmental woes in the Dorsey's living room, where only a few months ago, a developer had stared straight into Julie's eyes and told her he was planning to build a Neiman Marcus across the way, out here in the middle of farmland.

It was a lie, of course.

That was what had convinced Julie that the developers would tell her literally anything to get popular approval of whatever project they were trying to force through the pipelines.

Jess looked around the room, his blue eyes calling everyone out without any words. His implication was clear—it was time to move forward or just forget about it altogether. There was no way the thirty-somethings sitting in that room could continue their patterns of scouring public library records, making frenzied phone calls and attempting to keep track of and attend government meetings that were scheduled and rescheduled in an attempt to vote without public awareness.

"They're going to outwait us and get what they want—all it will take is the cost to buy two votes," Eric Johnson, one of the youngest in the room, said.

He was talking about what he and the others called the county commission. But the three-man group was, in fact, an old-fashioned kind of government called a county quarterly court, with the judge serving as a kind of county executive. Ron Simandl, sitting next to Eric, snickered.

Ron called the three county commissioners, Bill Tindell, Bill Deatherage and Jim McBee, "the three kings."

Eric called them "the three stooges."

Several people nodded at the idea of buying votes. None of them had proof that the commissioners' votes were bought, but what was painfully obvious to everyone in the room was that the commissioners were, as a group, incompetent, or at the very least, ineffectual and overwhelmed.

And the fact was, the time had come to either launch a full-out assault against that lack of concern and corruption or knuckle under. All of the people sitting around the living room had jobs. Lives. Children. For some of them, their spouses didn't understand their preoccupation with municipal planning. And there was only so long that spouses and children could understand late night meetings, frustrations and arguments.

Something had to give.

Jess's eyes rested on a thin woman with a blonde pageboy sitting across the room. Her name was Betty Dick, and she'd made it her job to personally give the county government hell.

She was too stubborn to lower her eyes when Jess looked over. He looked away first, and that was just the way Betty preferred her interactions to go. She looked out the window and tried to remember just how she'd ended up here.

Betty was a little too familiar with the inner-workings of county government, especially for a newcomer. She'd been following developers' plans for three or four years now, certainly more time than she'd expected when she'd moved to Knoxville six years ago. She'd followed her husband, Jeremy, around the country from her home in North Carolina. They'd gone to Tampa, Chicago and Boston before landing in East Tennessee. Now she was in nursing school, ready to settle into one place and raise her kids.

And because she was expecting to stick around, she'd become involved. *Involved* seemed like a four-letter word to a lot of people around here. The people who were *involved* seemed to cause nothing but trouble for developers who wanted to put in buildings without a thought to sustainability, and for politicians who wanted a larger tax base and maybe a few kickbacks.

So she'd joined the Village Green homeowners' association board. In fact, she was the vice president. And she'd taken it upon herself to watch out for the subdivision against those developers who wanted to grade out nearby hills to create valleys, which might be fine except that it caused her subdivisions' homes to flood. Their streets flooded every time it rained, and now developers were going one step further and actually building homes in the floodways.

Betty remembered the exact moment she'd decided she cared too deeply about the corruption and incompetence going on between the government and developers to just let things go. Three years ago she'd gone to a county planning commission meeting—that group riddled with developers pulling favors for their friends—and the chairman, Bubba Beal, had asked her, "Elizabeth, how long have you lived here?"

He had first-named her. She was Betty to everyone. *Everyone.* But he'd spoken to her like a child: *Elizabeth.*

She'd swallowed her frustration and told him she'd been a resident of Knoxville, and of the sparsely populated Concord area, for three years.

And then he'd said that wasn't long enough for her to have an opinion.

He had dismissed her just like that. And Betty had sat down. But not one month had gone by that Bubba Beal hadn't had to hear her voice or see her face. She had sat down that one time. But she would not be quiet.

Since then she'd become a regular sight at those meetings, watching out for the people in her subdivision, which sat amid vast tracts of farmland being sold to developers for pennies on the dollar. During those years she'd met other people with similar missions, and similar frustrations. Jess and Julie and Gene, Ron and Eric. Mostly men. She certainly stuck out as one of the few women in the room.

And now here she was, sitting in the Dorseys' living room after a particularly frustrating month and year dealing with strip development and eroding roads, all amid wild speculations that the city of Knoxville was going to annex all of Concord; and if that happened, all of her and her friends' watch-dogging would have been for nothing.

If Knoxville annexed, the city—in the midst of planning the World's Fair and desperate for a larger tax base—would have total control of zoning. The downtown politicos, far from rural Concord, would be able to put in any development without what Betty and the others considered proper controls, which would ensure new development didn't ruin old development. There would be no guarantee of common-sense measures that would prevent things like that new subdivision that was causing flooding in hers. Jess was right: the time had come to make the decision. The stars were aligning, and it was becoming increasingly apparent that drastic action had to be taken, or all actions should just be abandoned.

Betty sighed. Incorporating at first might seem great: this group creating their own government and forgetting those worthless planning meetings in downtown Knoxville, forgetting the phone calls to county commissioners and planners. But what an effort it would be, with no guarantee at all that any of it would ever come to fruition, or that any new city would be successful. Besides, Betty had a husband and children, was in her final year of nursing school. She had bigger fish to fry. Maybe.

Or maybe this was something that was big enough to take precedent. Maybe this was one of those moments where you pick something unsure and a little unsafe, and you commit to it because you have to, because you couldn't possibly do anything else; not because you know it's going to all turn out well. Maybe this was one of those moments when you stood up for what you thought was right, even if it is inconvenient and maybe if, when all is said and done, it's an absurd idea.

And she had never been one to knuckle under.

"Well, why not?" Betty asked aloud to Jess's earlier statement, her words tumbling out in curious overly round syllables, the product of her Southern upbringing and the time her father spent in Canada during the Depression.

Someone chuckled a little nervously.

"We could at least look at the whole idea. Do some research," Betty said, looking into the familiar faces of her friends.

A couple of the men—and a few of their wives—nodded a little more certainly, their mouths set in determined lines. Most of these people would no more sit down and shut up than Betty would; many of them were scientists and engineers, logical to a fault but deeply, deeply determined. Stubborn, even.

Jess smiled, quickly laying out the research he'd been working on for the past three years, outlining the work that would need to be done for any incorporation effort to be successful.

The first thing they'd need was money, followed by volunteers. Then they'd need to research the different kinds of government, and how to go about incorporating. That would call for a referendum, which meant scheduling an election. They'd need someone who could write out budget estimates for the new government. They'd need to decide just what that government would be required to do. And what they wanted it to do.

But most of all, they needed secrecy.

The worst thing that could happen was that Knoxville's mayor, Randy Tyree, and the city council, would get wind of their idea and go right ahead and annex them. Then there wouldn't be anything left to do.

By the time Jess was done talking, the idea wasn't much of an idea anymore. It was a goal, and everyone picked out a task.

The Carpool

May 1979

Ron Simandl walked out the door of his house in Linda Heights after he heard the car horn, stopping and locking the door behind him.

He stumbled a little down the front steps, tripping over his four-year-old son's tricycle, then righted himself and walked down the sidewalk that wrapped around the corner of his house and down his driveway, where one of his coworkers, Dewey Young, was waiting.

Dewey was an older guy, had flown as a bombardier in World War II and now was working for Y-12 in Oak Ridge with Ron and fellow carpooler Eric Johnson, where Ron was a chemist and Eric an engineer. Dewey had flown in a bomber unit with the highest casualty rate of any in the United States military; had once had to bail out of his shot-up B17, living to fly another day. Now he drove the carpool.

Ron dropped his briefcase into the floorboard of the passenger seat and scrambled into the car. The two took off down the street, Dewey's eyes magnified by his coke-bottle glasses, and headed down Chaho Road, their stomachs flipping when they coasted over a large dip in the street, where it had been paved to match the undulating terrain, rather than graded out properly. After a heavy rain, the dip held water like a pond, making it nearly impossible to cross.

The pair drove a block west, where they headed up the large hill at Peterson Road, up into Kingsgate subdivision where Eric lived. Ron hated this road. It had the worst blind spots of any road he'd ever seen, not to mention Eric had figured out it had a seventeen percent grade.

Seventeen percent. It basically qualified as a rock-climbing wall. Children sledded and skated down the hill when it snowed; some even broke out skis.

Ron's strong, square jaw clenched as they drove past one of the many blind spots on the hill and passed a man waiting to back his two-door sedan out of his driveway. The man's wife was standing by the mailbox in her bathrobe watching the traffic coming down the road to help her husband enter the roadway safely. Ron and Dewey passed her every morning. Every single morning.

Dewey waved.

Ron had moved to Farragut two years ago from Wisconsin and had quickly become shocked at the way development was done. He'd seen a subdivision go in where the developers paved directly over clay when they put the "roads" in. Of course the roads had begun eroding immediately and now were littered with potholes, cracks and enormous divots. When the people of Farragut made a big enough stink, the county would come out and patch the larger potholes. But the roads had never been repaved, never mind that they'd not been paved properly to begin with.

What was even more appalling was how things were passed through the three-person county commission and the developer-laden metropolitan planning commission. There weren't any long-term development or zoning plans in place, which is fine for the landowner who's selling his property to a developer, but not really for anyone else.

The three kings.

Dewey pulled into the cul-de-sac near Eric's house and honked once. Eric came striding out, thin and lanky, his gray eyes shining and his mouth set in a tight line. Eric was three days older than Ron, which put them both at age 32. Eric got into the car mumbling about his water going out, folding himself up into the back seat.

Kingsgate had been constructed so quickly and irresponsibly it didn't have the proper infrastructure to deal with all the residents. Eric lived at the top of the hill in Kingsgate, and some mornings he couldn't get water to his house in the insufficient water lines.

After dealing with his problems solo for a while, Eric had attended several meetings at the big Baptist church down the road for Kingsgate residents to drum up volunteers to attend county meetings and press the commissioners to fix their problems. He liked to think having dozens of people at those meetings helped, but it didn't, really. The more people from Concord came to the meetings with complaints, the less was actually done at those meetings. Instead, the commissioners would look out at the audience and simply postpone the agenda item in question. They'd do that over and over, meeting after meeting, until the size of the audience dwindled. Then they acted however they wished.

The three stooges.

Eric had begun taking Ron to those meetings at the church so he could address problems in Linda Heights, like the water that stood on the road after rains. Since then, they'd met other people in Concord with similar problems—more people than Eric had really thought would have issues problematic enough to lead them to drive downtown two nights a month. Or more. He'd met that tall lawyer, Jess, and the petite nurse with the blond pixie, Betty. And there were George and Julie Dorsey, who were chemists in Oak Ridge. They'd all been attending those meetings downtown for months. Or years, for some of them.

What was most depressing about those meetings was that he and his friends knew they were probably being treated better than the residents in a lot of other communities in Knox County, but things were still being done wrong. Developers were still allegedly buying votes on the commission, and developments were still going in without proper controls—homes were being constructed without regards to utility needs, roads were being paved without being graded properly and strip centers were being built without regard to zoning plans. Someone from Concord had to be present at every county meeting to speak out, and even then, things weren't being done the way they should be.

Maybe Eric and his friends were winning a few battles now and again, but they were losing the war.

Dewey slowed to a stop at the bottom of the hill and looked left across the main road that bisected Farragut, Kingston Pike—the road everyone was afraid was going to soon host commercial strip development all the way down each side. But this morning, Dewey, Ron and Eric couldn't see down the Pike through the sea of real estate, business and sale signs clustered on both sides of the road outside the windows of Dewey's low-slung sedan.

Eric muttered a curse and jumped out of the car, pulling up ten or so signs and tossing them into a ditch. Ron leaped out as well, and helped Eric clear the signs closest to the road, the ones blocking the view of any driver who would try to pull out there. But they were running late, and quickly got back in the car and pulled away. Dewey didn't say anything; the whole morning scenario, signs and all, happened often enough that it couldn't be counted as unusual.

Eric had moved to Concord in 1974 after a number of years in the north, moving from Illinois to Michigan and Wisconsin. And now here he was, five years later, wondering why no one in the county government wanted things done right.

Ron cleared his throat in the front seat.

"If you're going to live somewhere, you want it to look nice," he said, more to himself than to anyone in the car.

Eric nodded in the back seat, even though he knew Ron couldn't see him.

"I heard something the other day. They're thinking about putting some truck stops down on Campbell Station," Eric muttered, referring to the road that bisected Kingston Pike, and thus Farragut, in the other direction.

Ron's jaw clenched.

"What?" he asked, incredulous.

"Three. Three truck stops. Down there on the same road as all the schools. Truck stops next to the schools," Eric said, spitting out each sentence.

The trucks were a recurring complaint among Eric, Ron and the other regular attendees of the county commission meetings. Trucks looking to bypass the weigh station on the Interstate would take the first Interstate exit into Knox County at Watt Road—a little, winding, hilly, barely two lane road—and would toil up the hill, stalling traffic behind them. Then they'd come barreling down Kingston Pike at sixty or seventy miles an hour and take the Campbell Station exit back to the Interstate, past homes and schools the whole way.

And if those truck stops were built on Campbell Station, the problem would just get worse.

"That's ridiculous!" Ron exclaimed from the front seat, causing Dewey to jump a little. Eric grimaced. They didn't need to distract Dewey—his vision was so bad, he wasn't a very good driver to begin with. Eric had once seen him drive through a group of strikers at Oak Ridge, barreling through the men who had to jump out of his way.

Eric had congratulated him on "breaking up the strike."

Dewey had asked, "What strike?"

Eric sighed.

What disappointed him most about the whole argument with Knox County was the government's unwillingness to change. Only a few months ago, he and Ron and Jess had come up with a land use plan for the Concord and Farragut area. The plan laid out the types of zoning they felt should be used in the Concord area, with commercial in some areas and residential in others, separated by appropriate "buffer zones" so a house wouldn't be built directly next to a shopping center. They'd taken it to the Metropolitan Planning Commission, and in what had shocked pretty much everyone, the MPC had lauded the plan—drawn by "a bunch of amateurs"—and adopted it over a land use plan prepared by MPC's own staff.

Eric could remember celebrating that achievement. But then the county commission and planning commissioners began approving spot zoning on speculation, negating the very zoning plan they'd just approved. The whole land use plan had been nothing but an exercise in futility. It had turned out to be nothing but words on a map, a concession to the residents of Concord that ultimately proved to be worthless.

Nowhere in any plan were commercial zones for truck stops listed, but Eric knew that wasn't going to mean much.

He and Ron would have to tell the others and take this fight to Knox County. One more thing added to their growing list of complaints and problems.

One more reason to incorporate.

The Attorney

May 1979

His name was David Rodgers.

Betty could still hear him breathing into the mouthpiece of the phone. He hadn't said anything in a while, so his exhales were all she was going on to ensure she hadn't accidentally disconnected him. Or that he hadn't flat hung up.

David was an attorney, and Betty had been on the phone with him for several minutes detailing the idea of incorporating. He'd been silent while she spoke; occasionally he had interjected a question and sometimes just a comment. But mostly he had just listened.

"Well, what do you think?" she asked.

"I think you're crazy," he chuckled.

It had been a busy few weeks for Betty and the others. Everyone had taken off running with their incorporation tasks. Maps and statistics were being pored over; municipal and state laws were being studied. Contacts were being felt out.

But there was a problem.

Jess didn't want to be the group's attorney.

And once they went public, they would need one.

"I'm a behind-the-scenes guy," Jess had said.

And he was. Jess didn't like being the center of attention. He was looking up laws and helping as best he could, but he had his own law firm in downtown Knoxville. He was busy. He had too many clients, too many political allies and too many coworkers who could put him in awkward positions, and most of all, he did not have enough time to devote to a plan as big as incorporation. That had left the group with a big hole to fill.

They had to find an attorney, and fast. They would need someone honest and trustworthy and, above all, someone who could argue circles around that Knoxville law director, Jon Roach, if Knoxville decided to put up a fight.

So Betty had called David.

He was a young attorney who'd lived in Tennessee all his life; he worked for a law firm off Gay Street in downtown Knoxville—Kramer, Dye, McNabb and Greenwood. He was familiar with the area, the politicians and the laws. He lived in her subdivision, Village Green; he served on the homeowners' association board with her. David was a big guy with a sharp mind and an unusual way with words.

And he never wasted one.

David had a knack for always saying exactly what he meant and no more. And that's what he was doing now.

Betty shifted her weight in her dining room chair and swallowed against the silence over the phone line.

"Do you think we could do it?" Betty tried again.

"If you're asking me as an attorney, I would advise against it. It's going to be too much work and you'll get in over your head. But if you're asking me as a fellow citizen who might also be a bit bull-headed, then I'd say good luck to you."

He was silent again.

It wasn't an angry silence, not like the silence that seethed in the car after Betty and Jeremy drove home angry after those idiotic, wasteful county government meetings. It was a companionable silence—from what she knew of David, Betty estimated he was probably just digesting information.

But David didn't ask any more questions, and Betty didn't have anything else to say.

Instead, she asked him to attend the next meeting of concerned homeowners at the Dorsey home, the incorporation group. She wouldn't be in town, so he could go just as Village Green's representative. If, after hearing more about the whole incorporation idea, he felt that he could take on the task of being attorney, then that was great. If not, then he'd be doing her and the subdivision a favor by covering for her.

And Betty would be left looking for another attorney.

David gamely agreed to attend the meeting in Betty's absence, chuckling again, the sound easy, clearly something he did often.

Betty knew he could see through her game: that she was hoping once he heard all the problems the others had with the county government and the massive task ahead of them with incorporation, he would want to help. It was a desperate idea, perhaps, but David was the only attorney Betty knew who would be willing to put his heart and soul into the incorporation effort.

They needed him. There was no getting around that.

Betty hung up the phone, hoping David would realize that.

～

Betty spoke to him again a week later.

"I don't think you could do it," David told her.

His voice was kind, but he clearly was making no apologies about voicing his honest opinion.

David began listing the many and various laws with which the group would have to familiarize themselves and comply. He ran through voter registration book requirements, an archaic state law that would require the group to make a complete copy of all the voters registered at the election commission offices and then have each voter sign off on their own names in that new book. The new book would, by law, have to be held by an officer of the county government, called a squire.

That was another problem—the squire was a county official, and the county would certainly have a vested interest in one of its communities incorporating. If the squire decided to mishandle the voter book or make it difficult for voters to reach, that would be a difficult problem for the group to overcome.

And then there was the book itself.

Each voter's name would have to be copied by hand onto lists, then each list bound into a cohesive book that was left with the squire. If someone was left out of the book, they wouldn't be able to vote in any referendum for incorporation, even if they were a registered voter and qualified in every other way. Add to that the fact that the election commission would need a reason for why people were coming in with a need to copy down every Concord registered voter's name and address, and if secrecy were to be maintained, a believable reason besides incorporation would have to be thought of.

And finally, David had heard at the meeting that money and volunteers were becoming increasingly necessary. Volunteers could be found by calling friends or calling in favors, but the best way to raise money would be to go door-to-door. Those people would need to be told where their money was going, but could not be given so many details that if someone did decide to tattle, the entire cover would be blown. To avoid that possibility further, the doors that were knocked on would need to be chosen carefully. Area residents who might be opposed to incorporation would need to be avoided at first, until the whole thing went public.

"And that's a problem too," David said.

Betty cleared her throat, her hand covering her eyes as she sat at her kitchen table. She had been hoping David would feel the desperate need to incorporate, not focus on the interminable list of tasks that lay ahead.

But David continued.

Going public would cause a media hey-day. In the early '70s, a group had tried to incorporate Farragut and failed. A second attempt would be front-page news. That meant the Farragut Community Group would desperately need a spokesman, a frontman, someone who could speak to the media so different Group members weren't giving confusing, or possibly conflicting, versions of what they were doing.

And because of a state law, the group would have to be careful to avoid any scenario that would allow Knoxville the option of annexing after Farragut announced its intent to incorporate. That meant a careful selection of the new city's borders, not to mention careful timing. If the announcement could be made when the city would be forced into a slow reaction, that would be optimal. Betty could feel her heart sinking as the list of laws went on and on, and as David began reeling off scenarios and what-ifs she'd not even thought of. He'd clearly done his homework.

David slowed and took a breath. "And that's not to mention the fact that I'm not a municipal lawyer. I only know those laws superficially. I don't think you could do it," he said again.

Betty closed her eyes, her stomach clenching and heart racing. She shook her head, her mouth setting in a straight line as she stared across the table and out her back window, watching her children play in the backyard.

Just a block down from her was a street that flooded every time it rained, and yards that had been built in the floodway. About a mile down Kingston Pike was that Kingsgate subdivision with the crazy road that you basically needed a Sherpa to navigate. Something had to be done, and Betty was tired of people not listening. She was not going to back down now, not after she'd fought so hard in meeting after meeting with the county, losing more battles than she won. She would not give up before they even tried incorporation. So it would be difficult. That would be all right. Difficult was still doable.

She was still willing to put in the work, and if David wasn't, she would just find someone else who was.

"You're wrong. We can do it. We will do it," she said, her voice steely.

David was silent on the line.

"Are you in or are you out?" she asked, point blank.

There was silence over the phone for a few moments. Then David cleared his throat. Betty thought she could hear a smile.

"I don't know municipal law, but maybe I can learn it."

The Politicos

June 1979

Gene McNalley woke up one morning to see a county planning commission sign advertising a hearing just down the street from his subdivision.

That'd been months ago.

He'd slowly coasted down the hill from his home in Kingsgate and seen the sign for a new subdivision down Kingston Pike. Gene had groaned. He had known about all the problems with Knox County for a while, was reminded of it every single time he drove down Peterson Road with his foot on the brake the whole way, cringing as he rolled through every blind spot.

He didn't need to see another subdivision slapped in without proper grading or drainage or infrastructure. And then he'd discovered that the planned subdivision wanted their main entrance drive to connect to Peterson. The developers wanted their subdivision to connect to one of the most ridiculous and poorly built roads Gene had ever encountered…and he was a highway patrolman. He'd been down roads many people didn't even realize existed, and Peterson still took the cake. That week, Gene had attended a meeting at the First Baptist Concord Church for residents of Kingsgate to discuss the plans. He'd walked into the A-frame building that sat just feet off Kingston Pike a few minutes after the meeting started, still wearing his highway patrol uniform.

And then he'd heard his name from the stage. A friend of his had spotted him and nominated him to be Kingsgate's homeowners' association representative at future county commission and planning commission meetings.

Great. That's what he got for coming in late: meetings to attend downtown every week.

Gene—who was known by pretty much everything but his actual first name, Clifton—had moved to Concord in 1971 from middle Tennessee, after spending a few years in Germany while he was working with the Army Security Agency. He'd met his wife, Eva, abroad. Then he'd returned to Tennessee to work for the highway patrol and wound up in Knox County. He'd tried to stay out of all the controversy brewing in Concord, even though he'd heard the rumors about an incorporation effort. But there was only so much he could ignore. And since that meeting at the church, he'd been going to county commission meetings and planning commission meetings, encountering dozens of people from Concord and meeting up with one very familiar face.

Gene knew Jess Campbell from Democratic Party rallies and from common political allies. In a part of the county that was predominantly Republican, Gene and Jess shared ties that few others involved in the community activism in Concord—again, almost all Republicans—did. And sometimes, a different point of view meant that you saw the reasons for actions that others couldn't see. But even Gene and Jess couldn't see reasoning for some of the things going on in Concord, development-wise. It was just flat-out irresponsible.

Jess had been working with the Fox Den homeowners' association for a while, initially getting involved to oppose a strip commercial center across the street from Fox Den—the same one that had been billed as containing a Nieman Marcus. Jess had been working the system ever since, attending meetings and pushing for new regulations and restrictions. But he wasn't getting very far; nobody was.

Now the talk was that the planning commission was going to simply zone Kingston Pike for commercial development on both sides of the street all the way from the main interstate exit at Lovell Road to the county line. In other words, encompassing all of Concord and Farragut.

Gene figured it was the best way to take away any leg the Concord residents had to stand on—if it was all zoned commercial, then the county could put in whatever commercial development they wanted to, or whatever development their friends wanted, and say it was what they had planned all along. If they did it, it would effectively silence all of the Concord residents' arguments.

So Gene picked up a phone.

It was what he did when he felt backed into a corner, and it was certainly what he did best. Gene was a highway patrolman by trade, but he was a talker and storyteller by nature. He made friends easily; he kept secrets without effort and was fiercely loyal. Gene told great jokes. He loved to laugh, and people loved to laugh with him. And his eyes were very observant, trained from years of police work. He remembered faces and names, political ties, family members and even the stories people told. He remembered everything.

And he had lots of friends.

So when Gene picked up a phone, he had plenty of people to call.

Gene asked his friends, and friends-of-friends, pretty innocuous questions—he wanted to know what the planning commissioners were involved in, where their money came from, what they invested in, where they lived, who had pulled favors for them, who had contributed to their campaigns, what church they went to, where their kids went to school.

That night, he learned some interesting information. And over the next few days, his friends, and their friends, kept calling him back, remembering "one more thing."

Gene wasn't surprised to find out all the members of the planning commission had some type of conflict of interest with the one-stop commercial zoning plan. Maybe their property values would skyrocket, maybe their friends would be able to sell their land, maybe a developer was slipping them money under the table. If it wasn't one thing, it was another, and everyone had something.

Gene was familiar enough with the political back channels of local politics to be able to make his knowledge known. There were no threats and no blackmail; there was simply the knowledge that had been shared over a few nights' worth of phone calls. And in a small town, word spreads fast.

So, weeks later, Gene was sitting in the audience of the planning commission meeting, awaiting their ruling on the zoning plan. Whether the planning commissioners recognized Gene or not didn't matter to him. All that mattered was that they had heard someone was questioning their decisions. Gene smirked, his ice blue eyes twinkling, when the planning commissioners voted down the zoning plan without any discussion at all.

That was the end of that.

After the meeting, Gene walked out into the hallway and was promptly met by Jess Campbell, who was wearing a similar smirk. Gene wondered if Jess had made a few phone calls of his own. He wouldn't be surprised—they knew a lot of the same people, and Jess made friends just as easily as Gene.

But the successful vote-down wasn't what Jess approached Gene with: he walked with Gene to a quiet part of the hallway and then leaned over as if he were whispering a secret.

"We're going to incorporate," he said.

Gene scowled.

"We could use all the help we could get," Jess continued.

"I don't want another bureaucracy to have to deal with, Jess," Gene said, then turned and walked away. He considered that to be the end of the discussion. Gene was never rude on purpose; he simply did not want to deal with any new town. He was going to enough of these meetings; he was dealing with enough politicians and he didn't need any more of either. And Gene certainly didn't need any double government that would come with extra property taxes.

Gene simply wasn't interested.

And Jess should have known not to ask him for help again.

～

They met up again at a county commission meeting a few weeks later.

Jess approached cautiously, a fact that made Gene smile to himself. Not that he'd show it. Truthfully, he wasn't interested in incorporation, and nothing had changed that. But Gene was a talker, and he'd always enjoyed conversations with Jess.

Jess held up his hand as he approached, a small signal of peace, and Gene's eyes twinkled. Jess leaned in toward him again, still telling secrets. But Jess's tone had changed since their last conversation, and Gene detected worry.

"Knoxville's going to annex us, Mac."

Now *that* was news.

Gene instantly had a hundred questions, and he asked Jess several, but a county commission meeting wasn't really the place to talk. So the next day, Gene again picked up the phone. It wasn't that he didn't believe Jess—just call it double-checking, a side effect of being in law enforcement for years. Gene had to admit he was a little surprised to find that annexation wasn't only in Knoxville's plans, but that the papers had already been drawn up. All that was waiting was an impetus, a reason to have the vote.

And that changed Gene's options.

If the only options were going to be between being annexed by a city Gene knew well or incorporating into a municipality of a design he could have a say in, the options were pretty clear. The lesser of two evils would win every time.

So Gene sat back in his desk chair and mulled options for a while.

Then he dialed a friend in Nashville, asking about state law and requirements for towns, especially whether a town could operate without a property tax. Gene was surprised to find the answer was yes, and that answer gave him great relief. State law required a town to maintain roads, but towns did not have to provide fire or police protection or run a school system, as long those things could be provided by other entities. The county may or may not be willing to run the schools and the police department, Gene realized. But the possibility of a new town where zoning could be controlled and that could operate without a property tax was enough to make up Gene's mind.

He picked up the phone to make one more call.

Jess answered.

And, with his characteristic good nature, he offered Gene a chance, again, to help with the incorporation efforts for what he was calling the Farragut Community Group.

Gene said yes.

The Mall
and The Fair

August 1979

For Julie and George Dorsey, it all started with the mall.

West Town Mall was built in 1972, ten-or-so miles down Kingston Pike from the rolling hills and farms in Concord. It was a monster of a mall—four main anchor department stores with dozens upon dozens of smaller independent stores. And that mall had started all the commercial development on the west side of town.

Before the Interstate was built, Kingston Pike was the main road that guided drivers east-to-west through Knoxville. It ran straight from the heart of downtown to the Loudon County line. The Pike had once been a major thoroughfare, with cafés, diners, drive-thrus and hotels littering the way. It was seen in Robert Mitchum's movie, *Thunder Road*. When the Interstate was built, those businesses either moved toward the re-routed vehicle traffic or shut their doors.

The mall had turned that particular tide: it had become such a hub for shoppers that more and more businesses were locating near it. Subdivisions were being built near those businesses. More businesses were built to support the subdivisions.

It was textbook suburban sprawl.

And that was hurting the city of Knoxville.

The city had decided to host a World's Faire exposition in 1982, and mayor Randy Tyree had big plans. He had set apart more than seventy acres in central downtown as the site of the fair, and was busy with plans to construct a unique centerpiece of architecture he called the Sunsphere—a large glass sphere, golden, sitting atop a 200-foot-tall green metal truss system. A New York Times article in 1982 would say the architectural oddity "looks like a giant gold golf ball atop a blue steel tee."

To do all of this, he needed money.

And that was a problem, because with more and more people leaving downtown to move to the suburbs, Tyree's tax base was dwindling.

Thus, Knoxville had become notorious for finger annexations—annexing small areas of land, or in some cases, even individual pieces of property—most with the goal of increasing the tax base. As a result of all of these finger annexations, Knoxville's boundaries stretched out from downtown like the arms of an octopus. And to the average citizen, just where Knoxville began and where it ended was nearly impossible to track.

But the Farragut Community Group knew Knoxville's border already extended within five miles of the Concord area along Kingston Pike, and it wouldn't take much for Knoxville to push down the Pike a little more and have the growing tax base of the subdivisions being built in the evolving farming community.

"That's the start of the whole problem," George would tell his wife, Julie, all the time, pointing out the window to the general direction of the mall.

She nodded. None of it was news to her. She'd been president of the Fox Den homeowners' association for the past year and had convinced George to sit in her position for the next year as past president. He'd tried to stay out of the whole community activism movement of their neighbors in Concord. George had a Ph.D. in chemistry and worked for Union Carbide in Oak Ridge. He was a scientist, not an activist.

But now, here they were, holding meetings for the Farragut Community Group in their home, talking about the new city's borders and the incorporation referendum over beers in the living room. And here he was, enthusiastically backing their incorporation research.

"The more I look at it, the more it seems doable. It'd be stupid not to try it," George said to the group gathered in his home one early summer evening. Everyone was there that night.

David took the reins of the conversation for awhile, talking about his phone calls to area cities in Tennessee to get copies of their ordinances and building codes—looking at standards the new community might want to emulate.

At Gene's suggestion, the Farragut Community Group was looking at how to put together a town that would operate without a property tax, one that instead would use money derived from sales tax, beer tax, state-shared revenues and which would utilize federal grants. That was possible if the Knox County sheriff's office would agree to continue to provide police protection, and if Knox County schools would keep operating the three schools that would eventually be included in the new town's boundaries. The group still needed to get those guarantees.

Bill Etter, a friend of Eric's, was working on a budget, and was calling towns across the state, trying to get realistic numbers for state-shared sales tax and liquor taxes down on paper. That was going to be the best way to figure out how much fundraising the Group members would need to do on their own, besides money needed for the referendum costs, before any potential town became operational.

Jan Johnson, Eric's wife, and a group of women from Village Green were driving downtown several days a week and copying down voter's names and addresses for the voter registration book they needed to compile. Jan had told the election commission chair that she was hoping to open a business and was looking for a mailing list. Someone from Concord would copy down all the information onto a sheet of paper at the election commission office, then would bring it back to the Village Green clubhouse, where it was re-copied into the book that the county squire would keep.

It was a tedious and time-consuming process, and something that could not be mishandled if the referendum was going to be legitimate. As long as it was done carefully, that project was under control.

The biggest and most important project left on the to-do list was the task of drawing out the borders of the new town. The municipal borders couldn't be drawn within five miles of the Knoxville limits without triggering a state protocol that would allow Knoxville to have the option of annexing the proposed city.

And that was an option Knoxville obviously would take.

The five-mile rule meant some odd maneuvering on the part of the incorporators, since Knoxville's borders were hard to define, what with the constant finger annexations. Disappointingly, it meant two of the Farragut schools would not be included in the initial borders of the new town; they were simply too close to Knoxville limits. But the Farragut Community Group—which had named itself after the schools—had determined that if the referendum were successful, the new town government would annex the schools into the town immediately.

The Knoxville boundaries had been studied intently on maps and in legal boundary descriptions, then driven over and over again so they could be measured with car odometers. Then Eric and Ron had driven around the proposed town boundaries to measure them as well, marking the mileage marks on a map. Later on, those mileage marks had been traced out into the town's boundaries in Eric's den.

David was in charge of translating those black marker lines on the map into airtight legalese that would define Farragut's borders accurately to comply with county election commission and state requirements.

George smiled grimly around the room, at these people, most of whom he'd barely known only a few months ago, but whom he was now spending many of his evenings with. No one in the room was wearing rose-colored glasses anymore.

But they were still here.

The Leader

September 1979

By September, the Farragut Community Group was floundering.

No one had the time or energy to direct everyone else's tasks, making sure things were being taken care of in a timely manner. No one was willing to designate tasks and dole out the jobs no one else wanted. No one wanted to be the point person. And when the group went public, which was going to need to happen soon, no one wanted to be, or could be, the front man.

"We need a butt kicker," George told Betty after a particularly frustrating meeting.

The Farragut Community Group had accomplished a lot in a very short time, largely because the group was comprised of engineers, chemists, lawyers, a nurse and highway patrolman—all logical, scientific and deliberate. And they all were strong personalities: determined and stubborn. That meant they all had the independent drive to get things done, and so far, this had been a help rather than a hindrance.

But someone needed to corral those personalities into one cohesive group, a group that could accomplish more than the sum of its parts. Someone needed to be the boss.

And it really couldn't be anyone that was currently involved.

They needed a new set of eyes and ears; needed someone who wasn't afraid to come in and be the boss.

Betty didn't know who to recruit. David had been a great find, but Betty wasn't sure she'd get as lucky to have a second person walk into her life that would fit the exact bill. But the next week, she was at church talking to a couple she knew from Village Green, and Betty knew she'd found her man.

Ralph McGill and his wife, Marianne, lived on one of the subdivision streets that flooded when it rained and watched from their backyard as mounds of dirt were moved into the floodway in an attempt to raise it so more houses could be built. They recognized Betty from county meetings, coming over to tell about their latest run-in with the planning commissioners. Bubba Beal, the same commissioner who had told Betty she hadn't lived in town long enough to have an opinion, had told Ralph that he didn't have the right to speak.

Ralph, an engineer with a Ph.D. at Oak Ridge National Laboratory and a very purposeful man, had written out a list of dozens of technical, non-compliant issues with a new subdivision's site plans. Country Manor was being built near Village Green, and the improper grading and drainage was causing the flooding near the McGills to be even worse than usual.

Ralph had been reading this exhaustive list to the planning commissioners when Bubba Beal interrupted him: "Mr. McGill, there's another law in Tennessee that I think you should know about. It says that you're not allowed to speak here."

And that had been that.

Ralph had slammed his notebook shut.

"Fine!" he'd called out.

Ralph was normally extremely levelheaded, even to a fault. He'd been called "morose" and his taciturn expression didn't change much.

But Betty saw it changing now.

"So I just plain couldn't ask questions or say anything!" Ralph exclaimed outside the auditorium of the local private school, Webb, where their church was meeting, startling several passersby.

He and Marianne were incensed. Marianne even carried the photographs she'd taken of the flooding and the floodway construction in her purse.

"We need to fight back! This is ridiculous!" Marianne had said, her Texan accent carrying her voice further than it seemed her small body could take it.

"There's no representation. No representation at all. They don't care what we think. Don't even want to hear it! This crap has to stop," Ralph had said, his apparent irritation furrowing his brow.

"I've already decided. Next election, I'm running for something. Anything. Planning commissioner, county commission, squire. Something. Anything," he continued.

Betty smiled.

"I might have an opportunity for you, then," she had said.

The next Saturday night, she'd hopped on a bus at Farragut High School to attend the Tennessee-Auburn football game and had spied George and Julie. Betty walked back to their seats and leaned over to the couple: "I found our butt-kicker."

~

It was late when Ralph came home.

He'd been at Betty's for hours, talking to her and George and David—men Ralph recognized from their involvement downtown. But despite the late hour, Marianne was waiting for him, pouring him a drink as they sat at their kitchen table.

"What'd they say?" she asked as soon as he sat, too impatient to wait for Ralph to begin the story himself.

"She said, 'I think we can do better,'" Ralph answered, tilting the glass in his palm so the ice clinked. He looked out through the patio doors into the darkened backyard. Although he couldn't see it, Ralph knew the ground sloped gently to a small creek that flooded the bottom of his lot after a hard rain, as it did his neighbors' properties, and far too often, his street.

That was what had started this whole mess.

He'd owned this home for almost a year now—he'd moved into Village Green after accepting a job at Oak Ridge National Laboratory. And he'd watched the open, pastoral land around his home swallowed up by illogical and irresponsible development.

He was an engineer. He had no problem with development.

But it needed to be done right.

Ralph knew that in the daylight, he could see Country Manor in the distance, the bare red clay leveled out and washing into Turkey Creek with every rain. His mind quickly ran through the problems of Country Manor, the list he was never allowed to finish reading: the drainage system was completely inadequate; a local developer and home builder, Wallace McClure, was constructing just across the creek that ran through the McGills' yard. The land was much lower than the other side, and McClure would have to raise the level of his yard in order to keep the house from flooding. That meant that many truckloads of dirt were dumped in a floodway, something that was a violation of the law. The Federal government dictates the requirements associated with floodways.

Ralph remembered first taking his issues to the county government, a confusing conglomeration of courts and judges and planning commissioners. One county commissioner had looked over the map Ralph had set before him, pointed to the floodway, and said, "Well, we can just move that line."

Move the line? *Move the floodway line?*

Ralph hadn't believed it when he'd heard it. He had tried to explain that moving a line on the map wasn't going to help how a creek flooded in reality. But he'd never been able to get his point across. Every argument he'd ever had with the politicians downtown had been a waste of time.

Marianne cleared her throat, bringing Ralph back into the moment. She cocked an eyebrow.

"They want to incorporate," Ralph said, expecting Marianne to balk.

But she smiled.

Ralph returned the smile.

"And the question is, 'Do you think we should do it?'"

Eric Johnson

Eric Johnson's a movie and history buff.

That much is clear from the state of his den, decorated in Western movie memorabilia, posters of John Wayne and racks of DVDs—not to mention bookcases full of biographies and histories—against the walls. That den is where members of the Farragut Community Group would sometimes meet during those first months, mapping out districts and writing out the voter books.

Eric's wife at the time, Jan, now lives across the street in her parents' former home.

"You want to know something weird? Living across the street from your ex-wife," Johnson says.

His eyes are sharp and his smile is quick, cracking jokes left and right. The crack on his ex-wife certainly isn't malicious, and he lauds her later for her work on the voter books. Jan poured herself into taking trips downtown and back, over and over, to copy names by hand into a book for voters to check, he said. Jan also ran the Town's first census, a requirement before Farragut could receive any funding. Eric's jokes are unrelenting; the engineer is intelligent and his riffs are more than just knock-knock jokes. When he later served as an alderman, Eric would write many of the subdivision regulations.

"When the legend becomes fact, print the legend," he says of the incorporation story with a laugh, quoting from *The Man Who Shot Liberty Valance*, to which he draws several parallels to the Farragut Community Group's incorporation effort.

It's clear that he's thought of the incorporation years as a story for a long time; he's come up with names and personas for many of the characters—his friends and those he didn't agree with.

He calls the Farragut Community Group's near-constant disruptor—a man who opposed the election and who later was strongly suspected of harassing Farragut's first aldermen—"Liberty Valance," the title character of the John Wayne and Jimmy Stewart Western. Valance was an outlaw in the film; Farragut's own Liberty Valance was the Community Group's personal annoyance.

The group widely suspected him of harassing phone calls, made when Valance was drunk. He also was suspected of various stalking incidents, and even an attempt to run Eric over in a darkened parking lot. In later years, Valance—a long time resident of the Farragut area named Buddy White—sued the Town and won a re-vote to incorporate. He lost the suit and the vote—and a reported $250,000 in the attempt. But Johnson is quick to point out that White acted as he did not out of malice, but simply because he didn't want Farragut to incorporate. He'd lived in the area a long time and was opposed to the change that incorporation brought.

Johnson will drive you to a war memorial, relatively unknown, off a small street in Farragut, Evans Road. The memorial honors a Farragut soldier killed in Vietnam after he jumped on a grenade and saved those around him, earning the Medal of Honor for his bravery. The soldier is buried in a nearby cemetery. Valance gave the money to build the memorial.

"He was not a bad man," Johnson says, standing in a September drizzle at the memorial, his usual joviality put aside. "People should know he built this."

But get him back to telling the story of incorporating, and Johnson is back to remembering his cast of characters. "Redneckerson" was another member of the Concerned Citizens Committee.

Dave Rodgers he compared to Perry Mason, the hotshot lawyer from television.

"He didn't really worry too much about the consequences. He tried to keep things calm," Eric said. "They almost had to twist his arm to get involved. He was never overly impressed with himself. He worked with the town because he thought it was the right thing to do."

"But he didn't lose anything," Eric said of Rodgers.

"Poor Roach was embarrassed," he laughed, the surname reference to Knoxville's attorney, Jon Roach. Ron Simandl even drew up T-shirts in 1979 that featured a large boot stomping a roach, which Jeremy Dick had printed.

Dewey Young, the civil engineer Eric carpooled with, he calls Mr. Magoo because of his thick glasses. Gene McNalley was Buford Pusser, the famous "walking tall" sheriff from elsewhere in Tennessee. Ralph McGill was the cat to Bill Etter's dog. Or perhaps the other way around. Either way, they were always butting heads, Eric said.

"Ralph was too fair and objective," he laughed, commiserating. In the end, Etter, Gene, and even Eric himself would simply do things they thought needed to be done, whether Ralph necessarily approved—or even knew about them—or not.

"A lot of things were going on that Ralph didn't know about, and it's good that he didn't," Eric laughed.

For Johnson, the story of incorporation is all about the characters.

After all, it's not every day a group of engineers, chemists, attorneys, policemen and a nurse decide that they're going to become public servants and politicians.

Twenty Days

October 1979

The group now had a deadline.

Ralph had quickly taken up the reins of leadership, establishing time lines and task forces. And the first thing he did was decide when the group would go public.

1979 was an election year for the city of Knoxville. Randy Tyree was just winding up what was his successful reelection campaign, and Eric Johnson heard that the newly elected mayor was planning a recovery vacation in Florida. If the group could file papers with the election commission on the Friday that Tyree left, there was a good chance they'd have a decent head start before Tyree could return and the city could make its move.

But that date, October 26, was only a month away.

~

October 6

The first meeting with the full Farragut Community Group began with an update for Ralph.

David laid out letters between Knoxville city council members outlining plans to annex Concord into Knoxville limits. Betty had run across the original ordinance in the planning commission library downtown and had asked for copies of maps and plans. She had been shocked to find that all of the paperwork had been drawn out for annexation, and all it would require was a reading at a city council meeting.

It was no longer a question "if" Knoxville was going to annex Concord; it was "when."

The trips to the election commission office were continuing, with Jan, Betty, Marianne and some of the women who lived in Village Green and Fox Den copying the hundreds upon hundreds of voter names into a registration book.

The group had decided the registration book, once it was completed, would be left with one of two county squires who lived in the Farragut area. The chosen squire's name was Ted Lundy, and he seemed to be an honest guy the group members knew from Oak Ridge, and he was already making plans to keep the book at his home and making it available at the White Store, in the Village Green shopping center, a few evenings a week.

The other squire, whose name was Bob Hill, had been involved in the previous incorporation effort in the early '70s. The group figured that was just a button that didn't need to be pushed.

The book was almost complete, but it needed to be double-checked before it was turned into the election commission and then entrusted to a squire.

Eric, George and Ron had been going door-to-door to fundraise among people they knew, people who most likely wouldn't spread word of their efforts.

But no one really considered any of their work dangerous, even laughing when Ralph asked, "So are we opening ourselves up to physical harm with this?"

"This is the South. People are nice here," George had said. The only people he'd ever had problems with were the downtown politicians, and that had nothing to do with niceness, much less actual danger.

The new town's boundaries had been drawn out and David was in the process of translating them into formatted legalese that would be spelled out on the election referendum and in the ordinances that would have to be drafted.

Still to be done was drawing up a draft budget to present to voters and gaining assurances from county police and the school system that those entities would continue operating as they always had.

Ralph took on several of the tasks and doled out the rest, quickly settling in to his new role as leader.

~

October 15

The new town had a name: Farragut.

Farragut was the name of the local schools, with which the community was already strongly identified. They were jokingly called the "Farragut Farmers" at football games, and some of the other county schools would even fill the stands with hay when they played. But Farragut was actually a nautical reference, one to the U.S. Navy's first admiral, James David Glasgow Farragut, who had uttered the famous phrase, "Damn the torpedoes, full speed ahead!" during the Battle of Mobile Bay.

He'd been born nearby, but the geographical area in that part of west Knox County had never shared his name. It had been called Concord, or much earlier, Campbell's Station, after a historic inn that still stood at the intersection of Kingston Pike and Campbell Station Road.

Among the group members, there had been a strong push for Concord, since it was already how the area was labeled on maps and in history books. Concord had once been a marble mining area that had been flooded when TVA built its dams in the 1940s. Part of the historical Concord area still stood, but it was outside the proposed town's limits.

Ralph pointed out Concord was a startlingly common city name; there were dozens upon dozens of Concords scattered around the country. And the new town wasn't going to include the historical area of Concord anyway—it was too close to Knoxville. But Farragut, because of the schools, was already a familiar name in the immediate area. It was shared with businesses around town and was already something of a community identity.

So Farragut it was.

Ralph explained it this way—he didn't much like the name Ralph, but that was the name he was known by. So that was that.

Gene and Dave made a few calls to friends in Nashville and had strongly advocated the simplest form of government: one governed by a board of mayor and aldermen. One mayor would be elected at large. Two wards would be drawn on the north and south sides of Kingston Pike, and two aldermen would be elected from each ward. That idea went off without a hitch among the other members of the Farragut Community Group.

So now, the wards were being drawn up for the election commission, and the voters' names in the registration book were being divided by ward so they could properly register and vote on the day of the referendum.

～

October 22

By the end of the month, Bill Etter—with the help of Gary Head from the Municipal Technical Advisory Service—had come up with a prospective budget that used mainly state shared sales tax revenues and beer taxes to fund the basic responsibilities of a town—road maintenance, zoning and building codes and regulations, and the salary of a recorder.

Now all they needed were reassurances from the county school system, the county sheriff and the county subscription fire service that their services would remain the same, whether Farragut incorporated or not.

Bill announced his plans to copy the budget and stuff it into mailboxes. Ralph insisted he wait: putting out the budget before the group went public was too dangerous and would risk putting the entire movement in jeopardy.

Bill capitulated, but only for a while.

Ralph McGill

Ralph McGill is a quiet man with an intense gaze.

"We just were not happy with the flim-flam," he says, sitting in the formal front room of the home he shares with his wife, Marianne. They still live in Farragut, but no longer live in the home they were in during the incorporation years. They've moved away from the floodplain entirely, in fact.

Perhaps it's an unconscious move. Or maybe they knowingly picked their new home, situated on a hill, simply because there's not a creek nearby.

Either way, he and Marianne sit across the room from each other, remembering the frustrations of dealing with the county with exasperation and high emotions, even thirty years later.

"We didn't want it the way they were doing it," Ralph says.

"It was disgusting. We might as well have had no laws at all!" Marianne chimes in from her seat across from the sofa.

"It had to stop," Ralph agrees.

His voice never really rises, but there's the evidence of passion under the surface. Many wrongly have assumed—both during the incorporation years and in current political climates—that McGill is too stoic, nearly flat-lined. But maybe they've not heard him talk about incorporation or politics. McGill may be an engineer, but at heart he's a community activist, a politician in the purest sense of the word.

In fact, his devastation over the county's many variances and allowances to in-the-know developers or friends was the reason he became involved with Farragut Community Group in the first place. And his weariness of the same political figures controlling Farragut was the reason he'd later run for mayor, just shy of the Town's thirtieth anniversary.

The idea that activism is the way to get things done is a conviction Ralph and Marianne share, and their vehemence hasn't waned since the incorporation years.

The couple kept nearly meticulous records of their time involved in the incorporation and politics of Farragut.

In a thick scrapbook, nearly bursting at the seams, are newspaper articles, write-ups, campaign buttons and flyers and photos from 1979, 1980 and beyond. They also have kept photos of their home in Village Green and of the flooding in the streets—photographs of people wading down their driveways in water up to their knees. To Ralph and Marianne, it was never a question of not keeping these artifacts.

To them, the story of incorporation is a grand moment in history. A decidedly American moment. The Farragut Community Group's rebellion against the status quo of development in Knox County was a smaller, East Tennessee version of the Boston Tea Party.

"It was government without representation," Ralph says of the three-person county court government.

That's a notion you hear from many of the Farragut Community Group members—the representation for Farragut in county government was faulty. The east side of the county was where the power was at the time. That's all changed now. Farragut has the highest disposable income of any municipality in the state, and the town is widely known for its high-end residential developments. That's something Ralph and Marianne take great pride in.

But more than anything, Ralph and Marianne take pride in their work in changing a political system, in their own miniature revolution.

"We should be involved in government. If we aren't, we deserve what we get," Marianne says.

After the incorporation and early government years of Farragut, Ralph and Marianne largely disappeared from the public eye, until Ralph unsuccessfully ran for U.S. Congress against a long-time incumbent. A few years after that, he became Farragut's third mayor. The pair of them considers Farragut's incorporation a wild success, one that ultimately brought the county and the city into the future the McGills had tried to fight for all along.

"We brought everyone along, kicking and screaming," Ralph laughs.

As far as they're concerned, the county's and city's updates to their own ordinances are copies of what Farragut pioneered in the early '80s—the sign restrictions, zoning regulations and pedestrian greenways and sidewalks, among others—and, in many ways, they are.

Even the state has followed. When Farragut incorporated, it was one of the first municipalities in the state to require developers to put down a base layer of asphalt while developing and then to do a final paving after everything in the development was finished—a suggestion from Eric. Developers balked, but Farragut's first Board was insistent. Thirty years later, a final repaving of a completed development is common practice statewide.

Ralph and Marianne don't mince words when it comes to their opinions that Farragut has raised the bar for everyone around it.

"The thing to ask other people is, has Farragut been good for Knox County?" they say.

The Borders

October 25, 1979

The phone rang at Betty's house.

Again.

It had been ringing all night long as Ralph and Eric drove around town in a last-ditch effort to re-draw the Farragut borders, trying to prevent what was a small mistake from burgeoning into a huge debacle.

Earlier in the day, Eric had walked past a map of Oak Ridge, Knoxville and Knox County in a hallway at ORNL. Something about the way it was hanging grabbed his attention.

He paused in the hallway, looking over the roads, waterways and municipal boundaries, imagining Farragut's boundaries superimposed over the current lines and colors. And that's when Eric's heart turned over in his chest. The Oak Ridge boundary was probably no more than two miles from the very northwestern line of the Farragut boundaries the group had drawn.

They were too close.

Oh my God. We're too close.

The lines they'd drawn, the lines David had painstakingly translated to legal descriptions to satisfy the election commission—they were too close to Oak Ridge.

The group had been so busy trying to stay five miles away from Knox County's borders that they'd completely overlooked the Farragut border on the other side, straying within two miles of Oak Ridge.

And correcting that mistake was crucial.

State law would give Knoxville the chance to annex any new municipality—before it incorporated—if its borders were within five miles of the larger city. That same law also applied to smaller cities, such as Oak Ridge. And the radius around them was much smaller—two miles, rather than five.

So if the Farragut borders were within two miles of the Oak Ridge city limits, Oak Ridge could stall a Farragut incorporation vote. While it was doubtful that Oak Ridge would care about Farragut incorporating—they were in different counties, after all—Eric didn't want to take any chances.

He swore under his breath.

That year, Anderson county and Knox County had waged a very public war of words over a trash dump in Anderson, the county that was home to Oak Ridge. Knoxville dumped its refuse in Anderson County and Anderson officials were growing tired of the situation. Ralph could already foresee a deal in which the dump situation would be renegotiated in exchange for Oak Ridge stalling the Farragut vote.

He swore again, stalking to his office to make a quick call to Ralph.

They were supposed to go public tomorrow.

"We have a problem," Eric started, running down the situation with Ralph.

The pair talked about the press conference planned for the morning; the impossibility of postponing it.

"Let's just walk out the line tonight and re-type it all," Ralph sighed. "It'll just be a late night and an early morning tomorrow."

Eric calmed down, ended the call and went back to work. Later, he drove home and picked up the phone and called everyone else, trying to find who could help drive out the borders, correcting their mistake, on short notice. Betty volunteered.

That was how Eric and Ralph wound up driving up and down Watt Road in the middle of the night, measuring and re-measuring road distances with the car odometer. They would stop at the truck stops every half hour or so and call Betty on a pay phone with the new measurements. They measured every road, street and driveway, constantly referring to maps of Oak Ridge's borders that had been thrown into the back seat of the car.

For her part, Betty was sitting at a small writing desk she'd pulled into the middle of her living room. She would pick up the phone on the first ring, before it woke her children, and read out the mileage and road names to David, who scrawled them on a yellow legal pad. He would then spend a few minutes translating the directions into the proper legal language, and then double-checking it against a map that was spread out in the middle of the living room floor.

After he was sure it was correct, David stood up with his legal pad in hand and dictated the new language to Betty, who was punching each description into a typewriter. She gritted her teeth every time, carefully choosing each key. They didn't have time for her to make a typo and have to start all over again.

"BEGINNING at the point of intersection of the Southern right-of-way of Kingston Pike with the eastern right-of-way of Concord Road in Knox County, Tennessee, thence proceeding southerly with the eastern right-of-way of Concord Road to a point, said point marking the point of intersection between said eastern right-of-way of Concord Road and the southern right-of-way of the main line of the Southern Railway, thence westerly with said right-of-way of the main line of the Southern Railway to a point, said point marking the point of intersection between the southern line of said right-of-way and the Knox County – Loudon County line, thence northerly with said common line of Knox County - Loudon County to a point, said point on said county line being 2000 feet, measured along said county line, south of the point of intersection of said county line and the center line of the right-of-way of said Interstate Highways 75 and 40 a distance of 6000 feet to a point, thence at right angle northerly to a point in the northern right-of-way line of said Interstate Highways 75 and 40, thence easterly with said northern right-of-way of said Interstate Highways 75 and 40 to a point, said point marking the point of intersection between said northern right-of-way line of said Interstate Highways 75 and 40 and the eastern right of way line of Campbell Station Road, thence southerly with the eastern right-of-way line of Campbell Station Road to a point, said point marking the point of intersection between the eastern right-of-way line of Campbell Station Road and the northern right-of-way line of the Campbell Station Road and the entrance to the property of Knox County Board of Education up which is located the new Farragut High School, thence with the meanders of said northern entrance right-of-way and property line easterly, northerly, easterly, southerly, westerly, and southerly to a point marking the point of intersection of the eastern right-of-way line of the Kingston Pike entrance to the new Farragut High School and the northern right-of-way line of Kingston Pike to a point perpendicular to the point of BEGINNING, thence at right angle southerly to the point of BEGINNING."

All that to say, David explained, that the borders followed Campbell Station Road south to Concord Road, following the railway tracks to the Loudon County line on the west, turning north to the Interstate and then returning east back to the new high school, for which the Town was going to be named, and coming back to Campbell Station.

Ralph and Eric wrapped up their drive-by measurements in the early morning hours, coming back to Betty's to have a drink before they headed home, celebrating the fact they'd averted disaster. But no one partied too hard or stayed up too late—the press conference in the morning was only a few short hours away.

They could celebrate later.

Betty Dick

Betty Dick is a record keeper.

She sits at the table in her sun-filled kitchen, keeping an ear out for the phone to ring. She's expecting a call.

That watchfulness, that waiting, is apparent in her every move. It's part of her character, even when she's not waiting for the ring-ring-ring of the cordless phone in her kitchen. Maybe it's part of her training as a nurse, but her attention to detail is apparent in her every action. It came in handy for the Town in more ways than one—not only did she keep records of the Town during its pre-existence phase, she also wrote much of Farragut's very detailed and restrictive sign ordinance, one of the major ways Farragut is differentiated from surrounding communities.

She has a commanding presence. Her movements are timed to perfection, similar to the way a drill sergeant moves. Betty's voice is sweet and Southern, but it's clear she's a woman used to getting what she wants. She's a sweet-talker, a woman who can convince someone to do what she wants, what she thinks is best. Perhaps that's why she was recruited to convince both David Rodgers and Ralph McGill to join the Farragut Community Group.

And more importantly, it's probably why she was successful.

It's been suggested by nearly every member of the Group that without McGill and Rodgers, the entire enterprise would have failed.

There's an old expression that says, "Behind every great man is a great woman," and for McGill and Rodgers—at least as far as being convinced to join an incorporation scheme—that woman is Betty Dick.

You get the feeling, looking around her kitchen and through the orderly notebooks in which she kept records from the town of Farragut's incorporation years, that she is quite the Type A personality.

This is a trait most of the founders of Farragut have. Each is meticulous in his or her own way, recording their actions regarding incorporation almost by default. Some of them, like Marianne and Ralph, kept orderly yearbooks of newspaper clippings in chronological order, because they sensed even then that their actions might have a bearing on history. Others wrote out journals, dated references of their own actions and the actions of others, even saving napkins that ideas were scratched upon and bed sheets upon which political cartoons were drawn.

Looking at Betty Dick's orderly ledger book, with each expenditure of a Town that hadn't technically been formed yet nonetheless painstakingly noted, one gets the feeling she was keeping records because that's what she does. She was, it goes without saying, the Farragut Community Group's treasurer. Her notes in the ledger reveal the door-to-door fundraising the Group did: before the Town had been officially formed, it had a fund balance of $8,592.

She remembers David Rodgers carrying around un-cashed checks in his briefcase for months after the Town was formed but before it had a mayor to accept the money.

"The town literally existed in his briefcase," she laughs.

She also recorded the first time Rodgers was paid for his work with Farragut Community Group—January 25, 1980. He earned $1,620.60.

"He put his job on the line and wasn't making anything. Finally, they told him that he had to collect something for all his work," Betty recalls of Rodgers and his bosses at the downtown law firm that would eventually go by the name Kramer Rayson and become well known for Rodgers' municipal work.

Betty is also good with dates.

Days, months and even the order of things happening can blur over time, but Betty remembers the night she first told George Dorsey she'd found the leader the Farragut Community Group had been looking for, or perhaps more accurately stated, had convinced McGill to join the incorporation movement.

"It was September 29, 1979," she says with certainty. "The date of the UT-Auburn game."

The first Group meeting that included Ralph was October 6, she remembers, glancing through her notes. Following that were meetings on the fifteenth, twenty-second, twenty-fourth and twenty-fifth. The meeting on the twenty-fifth was the night the boundaries had to be rewritten to avoid being too close to Oak Ridge.

"We were up until the wee hours of the morning. It was quite an exciting time," she says with a laugh.

October twenty-sixth was the date of the press conference at the Village Green Club House.

In those twenty-six days in October, the Farragut Community Group drew up the borders of the Town and decided on the form of government it would be ruled by. Group members finished the voter registration book and turned it over to the election commission. They wrote up a referendum and requested a specific date, decided on the name of the town, wrote out a budget that reflected how the town would operate without a property tax. They began researching ordinances and deciding just how they wanted a new town to look.

By the twenty-sixth, it was time to publicly release much of that information. After months of hard work and various starts and stops, it was time to let go and wait with bated breath.

Betty smiles mischievously.

"Looking back, I can't believe we got all of that done. We were all young and stupid," she laughs again.

Going Public

October 26, 1979

It was 10:00 a.m. and there was only one reporter in the audience.

Ralph was standing in the Village Green Club House, readying himself to make the announcement about the Farragut Community Group's intention to incorporate, and only one reporter had come to the press conference.

Mayor Randy Tyree had left town on vacation, just as it had been rumored, and Ralph had already filed the paperwork to incorporate with the election commission that morning.

That action had been rather amusing—such early customers at the election commission office were rare, although no one there would have been exactly surprised to see them, considering how often they'd sat in the office copying voters' names over. And perhaps people in the know had warned a few of the commissioners. Perhaps even Gene or Jess. But the election commission staff had no clue what to expect when Ralph walked in that morning.

So when he turned over the paperwork and announced he'd come to file for a referendum to incorporate a town of Farragut, he was met with mostly blank stares and stutters.

But he had filed. The wheels were in motion. Now all that had to be done was making the public announcement.

And so Ralph had called all the newspapers, TV stations and even radio stations to announce the press conference. None of them had seemed too interested, not taking a bunch of homeowners with plans to incorporate an entire town too seriously. And maybe it was a good thing that no one was taking too strong an interest—it was rumored that in the first incorporation effort, the *Knoxville News-Sentinel* had taken such a rabidly anti-incorporation stance that the paper had singlehandedly ruined the effort.

That earlier incorporation effort had failed, in any case.

So now here it was, ten o'clock, and only one reporter was waiting to listen. Ralph would find out later that the rest of the reporters were, in fact, at the Club House; they were out back, smoking.

The woman sitting in the audience was Jan Maxwell-Avent, and she was a writer from the *News-Sentinel*. Ralph groaned. Of course she would be the one to show. Ralph cringed at the idea of a repeat of the earlier incorporation debacle. Unbeknownst to him, that wouldn't happen. In fact, Avent would write numerous stories about the incorporation in the coming months, all exceedingly fair by the Group's standards. They suspected she, at least, if not the entire editorial team at the *Sentinel*, was in agreement with the incorporation idea.

None of the papers wrote extensive stories about the incorporation effort until the first and second weeks in November. But by then, they were out in force—stories appeared in both Knoxville dailies, the *Journal* and the *Sentinel*; in the *Express*; in the west Knox County weekly, *West Side Story*; and in Anderson county's *The Oak-Ridger*.

"We want to set up a situation where this community will control its own destiny," Ralph told Dean Burgess of *Express*. "Governing officials would become much more accessible. Most likely they would be your neighbors. The people would be able to tell their governing officials what they want."

In a lengthy write-up in *The Oak-Ridger*, Ron Simandl told writer

Margaret Fifield, "There's a strong feeling out there to incorporate. We took a sort of straw vote and about 80 percent of the people in just one subdivision were for it. We've gone door to door and gotten out and talked to people. It's a very positive move ... the people just want to control their own government."

McGill told her, "This is a simple proposition; we have positive reasons. We want to simplify our government, take a step back to a smaller community and have our concerns listened to. Why be part of Knoxville and part of big city politics?

"We can incorporate and maintain what we have now without levying a property tax, unless the people want it."

McGill also outlined a few of Bill Etter's budget numbers: "We estimated, very conservatively, on getting about $500,000. The state funds are given on a per capita basis; at roughly $41 per person, per year. With a population of even just 8,000, that's $328,000. If we pro-rate the $12 million it costs Knox County to maintain all its country roads, and we have only 65 miles of roads to maintain. It means we would need $130,000. At most, we would need $200,000 for road maintenance."

McGill also addressed concerns that the sheriff wouldn't offer protection in Farragut. "The sheriff still serves the entire county. He wouldn't be able to enforce any ordinance we might make, but he still has to answer calls here."

And perhaps most importantly, McGill addressed the opposition that had surfaced in the weeks following the public announcement of incorporation.

"It reflects the generally held suspicion that if somebody does something there must be an ulterior motive. Their suspicions are unfounded," he told Fifield.

There was a feeling at the time that most proponents for incorporation lived in subdivisions, particularly the more expensive ones, and that many were not native East Tennesseans. Some were even

Yankees. Most opponents to incorporation tended to be big landowners and long-time residents of Farragut. Most were Southerners.

And those deeply generalized stereotypes did have some basis in reality, although, of course, neither generalization was completely true.

Depending on who was speaking, the Farragut Community Group either wanted to put a halt on development entirely or see Farragut built out and completely changed. But that overreaching generality wasn't entirely true either.

"We're not opposed to development; we just want to see it done in a more orderly fashion, and more clearly defined by what is obvious on other parts of Kingston Pike," McGill told the *Oak-Ridger.*

As Ralph and the Farragut Community Group saw it, their opponents either had development interests that would be hindered by an incorporated Farragut or were long-time landowners and farmers in Farragut. Either way, they were afraid of change: an understandable position, but one the group still hoped to fight.

PART II
The Battle

The Opposition

November 1979

Larry Vaughan glanced down at the phone in irritation.

It was the third time it had rang that night, as news about this incorporation effort was getting out, and the farmers and land owners who'd lived in the town for years were issuing a call to arms.

Earlier this week, it had been one of the McFees, the family who lived down the road from Larry, the road that was named after the very same family. The McFee patriarch had called in a panic, talking about the "outsiders" that were trying to incorporate little "one-horse" Concord into a town. And the McFees would be damned if they doubled taxes, causing them to pay Knox County property taxes and adding this new town's too.

What was wrong with the way things were?

That was the prevailing question among Larry's neighbors, the ones calling his home in the evenings looking for legal advice.

Larry was probably the only attorney they knew.

Not that he dealt with municipal law. He was mostly a general practice lawyer—writing contracts and handling divorces, and working with homebuilders and developers. And he wasn't exactly a long-time resident of Concord either. He'd moved to his home off McFee Road only a few years ago, in 1976.

Larry let the phone ring one more time before picking it up.

"Hello?" he tended to over-enunciate words, a practice he'd picked up in law school and just didn't turn off anymore.

"Mr. Vaughan?"

Larry nodded before answering in the affirmative, leaning back into his home office desk chair and closing his eyes.

"Mr. Vaughan, this is Anne Shipley. I'm Tom McFee's sister, Bill's husband. I'm a teacher down at the school," the voice, slightly tinny and noticeably Appalachian, said. Larry knew the woman, a popular teacher at Farragut Primary School.

"Yes, ma'am," Larry said, knowing perfectly well why she was calling. The McFees had lived in the area for years and years, still owning vast tracts of farmland that included the highest point in west Knox County, commonly called McFee Hill. Every year, the church down the road would run hayrides up that hill with a picnic waiting at the pinnacle.

"I guess you've heard all about this group, this incorporation thing," she said over the line, her frustration evident. "I can't believe that anybody would want to do that. Why would they want to do that? Why would they want to put in one more government that's going to raise taxes?" she asked.

Larry shook his head.

The more he'd heard about the incorporation effort—led largely by subdivision residents who had only recently moved to the area—the more he was wondering the same thing. And the more he learned, the more he wondered just why no one had heard about any of this before, why a project that had clearly been in the works for a while had been kept so secret.

"I've heard all about it, Mrs. Shipley. I'm not sure what's going on right now. I suppose we're going to be hearing a lot about it in the coming weeks," Larry said.

"I certainly hope not," she said, her breath huffing even over the phone. "Well, I think we should have a lawyer that agrees with us. They've got a lawyer, you know. Two. Jess Campbell and somebody Rodgers. Dave, I think. I just think we should do something about this."

Larry nodded his head again, agreeing.

"We'll see what they're going to do. It might just fizzle out on its own," he said.

Anne seemed mollified at that answer.

Larry might not be that familiar with municipal law, but he was familiar enough to know that incorporation was a difficult and frustrating endeavor. The truth was Larry thought the effort was unlikely to be successful. Frustrations with governments came out in different ways, and this move was easily recognizable as a release of pent-up anger with Knox County's government—a very understandable frustration, as far as that was concerned. But from where Larry was sitting, incorporation wasn't the answer.

Incorporation might reduce frustrations with Knox County, but it was only going to add another level of bureaucracy with eventual frustrations of its own. And that was if this Farragut Community Group was successful at all, and if they happened to avoid any number of potential lawsuits from the county and the city of Knoxville.

Which was unlikely.

Larry and Anne spoke for a while longer, sharing fears about how any new government might work, sharing the thought that things were fine as they were.

If a new town were going to provide normal services—fire, police, trash and that kind of thing—it would have to levy a property tax to pay for it all. And if it didn't levy a property tax, it wasn't going to have any services. Neither way sounded like a winning solution to Larry.

Anne hung up a few minutes later, vowing to continue to fight these outsiders that were trying to incorporate. Larry had the feeling he had been recruited. He didn't quite want to see a new government to have to deal with, and he certainly didn't want to see any additional property taxes. But in his mind, Larry could see the legal arguments that could be made both ways. And in truth, it was all just opinion: all "should we" or "should we not." There wasn't any right and wrong here, just feelings and opinions. Strong opinions, sure. But opinions all the same.

He left his office and returned to the dining room for dinner with his wife, Patricia, taking only a few bites before the phone rang again.

~

Anne Shipley called him back a few weeks later.

By this point, there was some form of news coverage of the movement nearly every day. Everyone was taking an interest.

And Larry's phone hadn't stopped ringing.

He'd found himself the spokesman for a group Anne was calling the Concerned Citizen's Committee, a name that fit a loosely organized group of long-time residents and landowners in Farragut. So now he was getting phone calls from concerned residents and from the newspapers. The *Express*, the *Oak-Ridger*, the *News-Sentinel*, the *Journal*; they were all calling, placing his quotes in contradistinction to quotes from Ralph McGill or David Rodgers.

The first one ran November 30th. Dean Burgess wrote it out in *Express*, and Larry had laid out his personal fears and the fears of the Concerned Citizens Committee.

"The only reason to incorporate is if annexation is imminent," Larry had said, referring to the commonly expressed fear by the Farragut Community Group that Knoxville could annex at any time.

"I would rather be a part of the city of Knoxville with services than part of Farragut with no services. I don't want to be a part of any city. More people would start coming this way, and I like living in the country. I'm against the idea of incorporation as it is now presented," he'd told Burgess.

But the whole idea was moving to a referendum, regardless of what

Larry or any of the concerned citizens thought. The paperwork had been filed; the train was already rolling. The only option for those who opposed the incorporation was to vote it down, an option Ralph McGill had wisely stated.

"If people can't find any merit in it, they should vote it down. They have the right to know the issues and vote for them," he was quoted as saying.

And Larry had to concede the Farragut Community Group was far more organized than he'd expected them to be. They were moving quickly and efficiently, more proficient than a typical grassroots movement. They even were planning community meetings at Farragut High School to answer questions for voters.

But so far, he'd not seen any assurances that the new town wouldn't levy a property tax, or that if they didn't, they would be able to provide adequate services. And he'd not seen any proof that Knoxville was going to annex. He could easily concede that it was a possibility; it was common knowledge that the city was trying to build its tax base and finger annexations were becoming increasingly frequent. But Farragut touched the Loudon county line, and Larry had a hard time believing Knoxville would try to annex this far out.

He'd believe it when he saw it.

Larry Vaughan

Larry Vaughan's office is a hodge-podge of papers, files and legal books.

It's not at all the stereotypical office associated with television lawyers with 800 numbers flashing across the screen, with orderly books stretched across wall-to-wall bookcases and a desk without anything on it. It is, however, the office of a man who is well read, inquisitive, even critical.

These days, Vaughan is a legal malpractice lawyer, spending his time suing other attorneys that have not lived up to their obligations to clients.

"I'm not a very popular lawyer with other lawyers," Vaughan laughs. He doesn't seem too concerned with that fact. And that largely sums up Vaughan's personality. He makes it clear, as he recalls just how he became spokesman for the Concerned Citizens Committee, that he was able to see both sides of every argument. And both sides deserved a spokesman.

The Farragut Community Group had David Rodgers. The Concerned Citizens Committee had Vaughan.

"There was a great concern there simply would not be adequate protection," he says, tilting his leather chair behind his desk and steepling his hands under his chin. "That became my opinion as well."

"A smaller concern was that a small group would run the area, and that the 'wrong' people would be in charge," he adds, making air quotes with his fingers, remembering the opinions of other members of the Committee.

"They had their points. But this was all a matter of opinion, not a matter of right and wrong."

Vaughan no longer lives in Farragut, not because of any high property tax he and other members of the Committee feared, but because the town developed so quickly. Vaughan and his wife, Patricia, favor rural settings. It's part of why they moved into Farragut in the first place. It's certainly why they left in 1989.

Vaughan does admit most people "came around" after the incorporation of Farragut, lauding people like Eddy Ford and Bob Leonard, who had opposed the incorporation at first but later ran for political office. People like Ford and Leonard, he said, helped bridge the gap between those who had wanted nothing to do with any town of Farragut and then were expected to live in one. Ford and Leonard also became two of the town's staunchest advocates, fighting lawsuits and calling in favors of their own to ensure its success in those early years.

But Vaughan, ever observant, also notes the commonly criticized aspects of the town, particularly its sign ordinance.

"Many builders stopped working in Farragut just because they thought it wasn't worth the hassle, especially in those first five to ten years." Vaughan, in his long tenure as an attorney, has held a general practice and specialized in construction law. He differs from many who criticize Farragut for being too stringent with its rules: he doesn't speak hearsay. He knows the builders he speaks of, remembers clearly their refusal to build in the Town and their many complaints to him.

"And, you know, there was a certain price range of homes that weren't allowed in Farragut. The perception was that they were an uppity, snooty bunch of people."

"But that's not where Farragut is any more."

The Volunteers, The Letters and The Voters

November 1979

By the time the newspapers were running stories about the incorporation effort, the Farragut Community Group had more than fifty volunteers.

Those volunteers were going door-to-door, collecting donations and offering to answer questions, scheduling meetings with groups of homeowners and subdivision associations and planning large public meetings to be held at the high school.

And Bill Etter figured that now was the time to disseminate the budget estimates he'd drawn up, with or without Ralph's permission. Bill had called several local cities, small and large—including Brentwood, Berry Hill, Goodlettsville and Oak Hill, among others—to find out the revenue projections Farragut could expect for its size and population. The three largest sources of revenue for the new town, if it didn't levy a property tax, would be state-shared tax, sales taxes and beer taxes.

And it was a lot more money than anyone had expected.

Etter estimated the Farragut government would bring in about $595,000 each year from sales tax shares and federal revenue sharing, the state's Hall income tax, business tax and beer tax. With a bare-bones government—just administration, road maintenance and insurance, plus things like legal and engineering fees—Farragut would spend about $312,000 a year.

The Farragut Community Group estimated they could just pay for county police and subscription fire protection, rather than starting up a fire department and police department of their own. In other words, Betty had said, operating a town would be totally feasible, even without a property tax, which would be most people's biggest fear about incorporation.

And Bill was going to prove it to them.

One night in early November, he drove out and stuffed mailboxes with copies of his two-page budget, then slid copies of the budget under the doors of the newspapers and television stations. With it, Bill included an explanatory letter.

"A citizens group of the Farragut area filed for incorporation on October 26, 1979. Previously, petitions were signed, funds raised and legal papers prepared with the quiet support of over 300 citizens within the community. Now that the petition is filed, all citizens within the proposed Town of Farragut boundaries will have a voice in determining their local government. A referendum is requested for December 11, 1979, but is subject to approval of Knox County Election Commission," Bill wrote in the letter.

And Bill addressed what he knew was a concern—the fact that some people considered the secrecy attached to the plan a personal affront.

"It was impossible to contact everyone before filing the qualifying petition. Now that it has been filed, personal contacts and information community meetings will follow. The support of all residents is requested," he wrote.

Bill also included a write-up of the proposed Farragut boundaries and a description of the mayor-alderman form of government.

The information quickly made the rounds, and soon county squire Ted Lundy was busy signing up registered voters at The White Store, where he'd set up shop on Saturdays and in the evenings with the voter registration book. By law, only Lundy could hold the voter book and only he could check that each voter was registered with the Election Commission and listed in the book.

And it was during that process that the Farragut Community Group learned of one of its biggest mistakes.

When the names had been copied from registered voter lists at the downtown Election Commission office, then copied again into the voter registration list, a whole group of residents had been inadvertently left off.

Ralph was furious. Briar Creek Drive, an entire street inside Village Green, wasn't included on the list. There had been confusion over the name of the street; the name led a few of the copiers to think the street was in Sweetbriar, which wasn't being included in the borders. A few voters along Evans Road and Turkey Creek Road also were accidentally left off. That meant that even registered voters who lived on those streets wouldn't be allowed to vote in the referendum. And the Concerned Citizens Committee was looking for any technical error as an excuse to prevent the referendum. Ralph didn't need these kinds of mistakes, and didn't need rogue members of the group disseminating information without permission.

They needed to be one front; that was why Betty had recruited Ralph in the first place.

Larry Vaughan certainly wasted no time delivering his own letter, breaking down each line of the budget and refuting Bill Etter's calculations. Farragut wouldn't collect more than $500,000 a year; Vaughan said. A city of 7,500—and Farragut had about 6,000 residents—only collected an average of $298,200 in all of the applicable taxes Farragut could receive.

Vaughan recalculated expenditures too, including salaries for a judge and police officers, arguing that the Knox County Sheriff's Office was unlikely to continue operating in another city in which it had no jurisdiction. Expenditures came in at $437,000, Vaughan wrote.

"It is felt that based upon the revenues that the City of Farragut could expect as compared to the expenses that would be incurred, that the City could not maintain services or even existence," Vaughan's letter said.

"We of the Concerned Citizens Committee encourage every citizen to gather all information he or she can gather concerning the proposed incorporation. We would encourage you to make sure that the sources of information are accurate and non-biased," he closed.

Ralph was still trying to figure out the best method of damage control when Bill Etter mailed out another letter, telling residents of Village Green that feedback the Farragut Community Group had received indicated nearly eighty percent of the subdivision residents supported incorporation.

"Unfortunately this issue is becoming very emotional and political in some areas. Although some large landowners are in favor of the incorporation, leadership of the opposition is primarily a few large long-time landowners and land developers (some of which do not live in the area). A few of the big land owners have implied that because they have lived in the area all their life and since they own more property than anyone else, they should have more voting power than subdivision people or small rural land owners. This group is passing out false rumors in many neighborhoods and in our schools in an effort to gain opposition to the referendum," Bill wrote in his letter.

After that, the mail-outs stopped. The incorporation and opposition forces largely relied on word-of-mouth from there out, not to mention the ever-more-frequent news articles being printed in each of the area newspapers.

The Farragut Community Group began throwing its energy into its planned community meetings, and Ralph and Bill only had one more tiff.

Ralph, it was assumed, would lead the community meetings, acting as emcee and answering questions. He'd been the face of the group for weeks, after all. But one night, Bill called him and requested that he allow other people to lead the meetings.

"Why would that be?" Ralph asked.

"Because you're too morose," Bill said. "People are emotional about this, and we need someone who's going to show his passion about it too."

Ralph fumed for a night before finally taking the recommendation under advisement, and for the most part, Jess and David led the community public information meetings.

Bill and Anne Shipley

Anne Shipley was a first-grade schoolteacher, and her husband, Bill, worked for the telephone company. They'd grown up in Concord; their families had been there for years and years.

And as far as they were concerned, the changes the Farragut Community Group was making were just flat-out unwelcome.

"We were living here and had lived here all our lives. We were a farming community. The people in the community had put in a telephone system that was fine and then they came along and the community did a water system with First Utility District, which was done by people in the community. And we just didn't see any real need to incorporate when things were going very well the way they were," Anne says.

She and Bill still live in their home off Smith Road in Farragut, although the land around them is no longer farmland. Churches, subdivisions, drugstores and gas stations are their immediate neighbors now.

"We had the best schools in the county and the best of everything going for us, so why did we need the incorporation?" Anne asks.

That seems to be the shared thought of many of the residents who were against incorporation. They simply didn't see why it was necessary. The community was the one they'd always lived in. For them, nothing had changed. Nothing was needed.

And there was the fact that a lot of the subdivision dwellers, including nearly every member of Farragut Community Group, weren't from the area, weren't from the state, weren't even Southerners.

"There were a lot of us who felt like we had a lot of northerners coming in trying to make us like what they had in New Jersey, New York and Chicago and all these other places," Anne says.

Anne doesn't remember leading the charge to start the Concerned Citizens Committee, as Vaughn says she did, but she concedes it was entirely possible. "I guess when I think back on it that, yes, that's probably right," she laughs.

Most of her family members were against the incorporation; in fact, she remembers all of the McFees being opposed except her brother, Tom. Between the incorporation effort in the early 1970s and the Farragut Community Group effort in 1979, Tom changed his views on incorporation, although Anne doesn't remember why.

Once the incorporation effort turned out to be successful, Anne and Bill recall the politically charged efforts to find candidates for mayor and aldermen positions. Bill remembers climbing up telephone poles and hanging campaign posters out of reach so they couldn't be torn down. Ultimately, Bill decided to run for mayor against Jan Johnson, Bill Etter, Ted Lundy and Bob Leonard.

"See, I was working with the telephone company at that time and was in about everybody's house and at that time I knew a lot of people. So that's the way I got involved," Bill remembers.

"At that time, this place was very small," he added.

Bill eventually would withdraw from the mayoral race, a decision Anne and Bill recall as being done in concert with Leonard in an effort not to split the vote.

"We was not going to get enough; we were going to split the votes. So I told Bob, I said, "Bob, you go ahead and run and I'll withdraw and that will prevent the split vote," Bill remembers.

Bill and Anne were good friends of Eric Johnson's Liberty Valance, whose name was Buddy White.

"He practically grew up with Anne's family. He stayed at their house more than he did at home. Buddy was a small businessman and he felt like the place was too small and what they wanted was to get a lot of people settled in who weren't familiar with the county or the area, and they was going to run it to suit themselves and make rules and regulations for business mainly," Bill says.

"And he felt like the people in the community had governed themselves pretty well and had got along right well with Knox County and what have you, and he wanted to avoid a lot of red tape, since he was a business man.

"He wasn't for it," he added simply.

And that's the end of it, as far as the Shipleys are concerned.

The incorporators weren't community minded: at least not mindful of the community as the long-time residents saw it, as they had seen it growing up. The incorporators were newcomers coming in and wanting to change too much, too quickly. Not many of the long-time residents jumped on board quickly, if at all. Anne's brother Tom was one of the exceptions. Another member of the family, Mary Nell McFee, later became involved with Farragut's Folklife Museum and even had a gallery in the museum named for her.

"The rest of us basically were against it," Anne says.

The Public Meetings

November–December 1979

After the papers had been filed, the biggest task was convincing the community that incorporation could work.

The Farragut Community Group first held meetings in the Village Green and Fox Den clubhouses, inviting people to come by going door to door. Mary Lou Koepp—who later would become Farragut's first employee—and her husband, Tom, attended the meeting in Village Green. Tom had been recruited by Ralph to go door to door and invite others on their street.

Rodgers and McGill led that meeting, answering questions and explaining the responsibilities of the Town: largely road maintenance and codes enforcement. Mary Lou noticed Bob Leonard, who lived a few streets over from her.

"If it ain't broke, don't fix it," he called out from the row behind her.

She knew him, of course; as did most people. He lived a few streets over from her. And now it was no secret that he was against the incorporation.

Later, the Group began holding public meetings at Farragut High School one evening a week, where they would answer questions about the ins and outs of incorporation. Mostly, David or Jess spoke, but everyone else sat in the audience and only occasionally stood up to give their opinions. The first meetings weren't well attended, besides by the media, but by the end of the month, 150 or 200 people were attending each one.

The group had finally received confirmations from the sheriff, Joe Jenkins, and the county school superintendent, Earl Hoffmeister, that each of those entities would continue services to Farragut residents regardless of incorporation. While the members of the group had long hoped that would be the case, the official announcement was still quite a windfall. It was now certain that any new town wouldn't have to pay for two of the most expensive departments a municipality could operate— police protection and education.

In fact, Hoffmeister seemed downright in favor of incorporation.

The *West Side Story* wrote, "Hoffmeister stated that if the Farragut community fails to incorporate and when the City of Knoxville annexes the area, students from the Farragut area face the prospect of being bussed to the Knoxville inner city schools. He indicated that this was a very real possibility because of economic considerations."

"Incorporation will not change anything with the schools unless Knoxville annexes to the Farragut city limits, taking in the Middle and Intermediate Schools. There would be problems and legally the city could charge tuition," Hoffmeister later told the *News-Sentinel*.

Ralph seemed to think Hoffmeister wanted to avoid a problem with the Knoxville schools and was simply taking the easy way out—for him, a Farragut incorporation was simply a continuum of the status quo.

And that was the way Jenkins saw it, too. "I'll give the same service they get now, if they incorporate," he told the *News-Sentinel*.

It was at one of those later, crowded meetings that a grizzly old

In these photos taken by Ralph McGill,
Village Green streets flooded in July 1979.

Farragut Community Group members assembled in
Eric Johnson's basement, from left, are Ralph and Marianne
McGill, Eric Johnson and Ron and Wanda Simandl.

During a dialogue commemorating the Town's 30th anniversary
in 2010 are Farragut Community Group members, from left,
Ralph McGill, Eric Johnson, Gene McNalley, David Rodgers,
Betty Dick and Ron Simandl.

Ralph McGill in 1980.

Betty Dick in 1987.

Gene McNalley and his wife, Eva, enjoy a party at Eric Johnson's home.

Bill Etter sits with members of Farragut Community Group
in Eric Johnson's basement.

Gene McNalley in the Tennessee Highway Patrol office.

Jan Johnson relaxes with Farragut
Community Group members during a
party at her home.

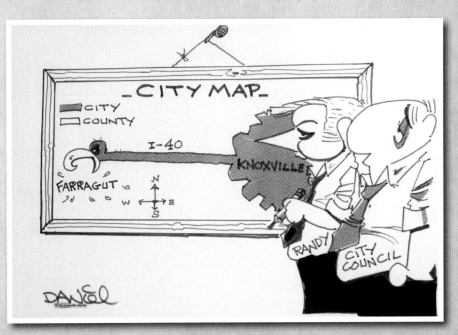

Knoxville political cartoonist Charlie Daniel drew a number of
editorial illustrations for *The Knoxville Journal* during the 1979
and 1980 incorporation movement — like this one depicting the
city as a vulture consuming Farragut. Daniel later gave original
copies of those Farragut cartoons to Mayor Bob Leonard,
who hung them in his home office.

"Damn the torpedoes ... full speed ahead!" cries Farragut as it faces city council, lawsuits and Knoxville mayor Randy Tyree.

Mayor Randy Tyree "fishes" off the I-40/I-75 pier as Farragut swims past.

George Dorsey, at left, and David Rodgers showcase
the Town of Farragut's charter in front of the state
capitol building in Nashville Jan. 16, 1980.

David Rodgers hands the Town of Farragut's
charter to a state clerk Jan. 16, 1980.

Ralph McGill shows of the
Town of Farragut's charter
in January, 1980.

City Council catches its
britches on Farragut's
barbed-wire fence.

Knoxville, Knox County and Farragut make a second attempt at working together as the Three Musketeers.

Marianne McGill and her son, Norm, celebrate the successful incorporation vote with T-shirts depicting a boot stomping on a roach above the words, "We did it."

Mayor Bob Leonard during a Board of Mayor
and Aldermen meeting in 1987.

**ANCHOR FARRAGUT
SECURELY**

WITH

A TIE TO TRADITIONS

RESPONSIVE

GOVERMENT

**REASONABLE GOVERNMENT
WITH HONESTY AND
INTEGRITY AND CONCERN**

**ELECT
MARIANNE M^cGILL**

**ALDERMAN - 2 YR. TERM
NORTH WARD
FARRAGUT ELECTION
APRIL 1, 1980**

Marianne McGill's election cards for the 1980 election touted her desire
to "anchor Farragut securely" through "reasonable government with
honesty and integrity and concern for everyone."

Eddy Ford makes his point during a Board of Mayor and Aldermen meeting in 1984.

Cartoonist Charlie Daniel wrote a personal note to new Mayor Bob Leonard: "Best wishes to the new incumbent."

Mary Lou Koepp, Farragut first full-time employee and Town recorder from 1980 to 2004, sits during her retirement party with husband, Tom.

Farragut's first Board of Mayor and Aldermen is pictured with Farragut's first staff members in June 1981. In the front row, from left, are aldermen Marianne McGill and George Dorsey, Mayor Bob Leonard and aldermen Eddy Ford and Eric Johnson. In the back row are Bill Maney, David Rodgers, Mary Lou Koepp and Jack Hamlett.

Arguments over the incorporation and eventual borders
of the town of Farragut continued for years.

Eddy Ford and his wife, Linda, react to Eddy's final victorious
election to the Town's mayoral post in 2005.

Bob Leonard visits Town Hall with his wife, Marie,
for a Christmas celebration in 2009.

Ralph McGill is sworn in
as Farragut's third mayor
in 2009.

George and Julie Dorsey attend an event commemorating
the Town's 30th anniversary in 2010.

Eric Johnson took a backseat
to politics after his stint on
Farragut's Board of Mayor
and Aldermen.

Jess Campbell remained involved in Farragut community events and even in development until he passed away in 2010.

politician showed up and quietly sat down the aisle from Ron Simandl.

Sitting quietly was not a normal thing for the man, who was infamous for punching a fellow Knoxville city councilman in the 1950s. A photograph of the incident even ran in *Life Magazine*. He had voluntarily retired from politics in '71, but had remained active in local circles. Now he mostly ran his chain of grocery stores, including one in Farragut.

Cas Walker had sat quietly through the meeting, listening to the discussions back and forth about incorporation, the questions and the answers, the back-and-forth between the Concerned Citizens and the Farragut Community Group. And mostly, he'd gone unnoticed.

David had just announced that the FCG wouldn't take any more questions when Jess looked out and spotted the man. Impetuously, he called him up on stage, announcing he saw a "pretty good politician," and was curious what that man had to say. Jess knew he might regret that decision, especially if someone as influential as Cas spoke out against incorporation. He tried not to look down the stage at Ralph, who was frowning at him.

The auditorium buzzed as Cas stood at his seat and acknowledged the invitation with a jaunty tilt of his head.

Jess swallowed. God only knew what Cas was going to say.

The older man shuffled up the auditorium steps and walked down the stage to the microphone. He cleared his throat and threw out a sly smile, ever the salesman. A bit of laughter rolled around the auditorium, and Jess smiled nervously out at the 200-or-so people sitting in the high school seats.

"You've got the most expensive land in any part of the whole Knoxville area," Cas said.

"And we don't need no annexing in this area," he said, thumping his fist on the lectern. Two of the man's Cas Walker Cash Stores sat nearby. And while Cas had been on city council for years, it was no secret that property taxes were higher in the city, and if the city annexed Farragut, Cas would have to pay them.

Jess smiled, relief bubbling in his chest.

Cas was ever the logical businessman.

The older man leaned into the microphone and cautioned the rest of the audience not to be too concerned with any new town's services, saying the county could handle many of the things the Concerned Citizens Committee worried about, echoing earlier proclamations of service from Hoffmeister and Jenkins.

And that's when Cas paused, readying the audience for his dramatic, no-guts, no-glory final proclamation, the one that made headlines the next day and ended the meeting.

"You know, everyone wants to get to heaven. But no one wants to die to get there."

~

Most of the high school meetings were fairly peaceful, especially at those where county officials, including the sheriff, were present. But the Concerned Citizens Committee began making their presence known, and while those debates could become rather heated they were never violent. The problem was a few of the "old-timers," as members of the Farragut Community Group called them: property owners who had lived in Concord their entire lives, whose families had lived here for generations, who had seen Concord when the closest traffic light was in downtown Knoxville, before Kingston Pike was even a two-lane road, before TVA had flooded the old marble quarry with its dams.

Those were the people who were most emotional about incorporation. A few of those people could cause problems, especially if they'd been drinking, which was sometimes the case.

One night after a mostly uneventful meeting, Eric Johnson was walking out to his car in the high school parking lot, taking his time and thinking about other things. He looked up at the sound of squealing tires and stepped out of the way just as a car raced past him, narrowly missing him in the dark parking lot.

Eric didn't have to see the license plates to know who the driver was.

"Valance," he muttered, the nickname he had for one of the local old-timers who frequented the meetings, often drunk, and routinely made his opposition to incorporation known.

The same car and driver turned up a few minutes later, this time tailgating Ralph down Kingston Pike, the driver weaving in and out of the lane and revving his engine. Ralph kept driving past his street in Village Green, not wanting to lead any drunken maniac to his home, his wife and his kids. He parked in a stranger's driveway and waited for the driver to leave.

Even after that, Ralph kept driving around the subdivision and the rest of Concord, making sure he wasn't being followed. He drove home and locked all the doors. Then he checked them. Twice.

When he and Eric spoke a week later, Eric told him he was carrying a gun in his car and confirmed Ralph's own suspicions about the driver. A few days later, Gene heard about the trouble after the meeting. He asked a friend of his who worked with the Tennessee Bureau of Investigation to watch over Ralph's house, which he did for the rest of the incorporation effort.

He never told Ralph, figuring that some things didn't need to be said and might just cause more worry than help.

At the next public meeting, Jess and Gene called in a few more friends to help ensure the meeting—and its aftermath—remained orderly. Gene asked off-duty THP officers to make a stop at the meeting, while Jess recruited several members of the Teamster's Union, which he represented in various legal affairs.

They were all big, big men.

All Jess and Gene asked them to do was sit silently in the audience, a task they performed with wild success.

And after that, there weren't any more scares in the parking lots after meetings.

Gene McNalley

Gene McNalley is a storyteller.

A conversation with him, especially one that puts him in the role of entertainer, is bound to be a long one. And he's honest, often brutally so. McNalley was a long-time police officer and doesn't play many games. But he does like to laugh.

"I agreed to join the Farragut Community Group as the lesser of two evils," he chuckles, his bright green eyes shining from behind his glasses. Knoxville's plans to annex were the worst of those evils, and Gene is clear that only when annexation or incorporation were his two options did he decide incorporation was the way to go. Before that, he was just one more Kingsgate citizen fighting haphazard development.

McNalley was dragged into the incorporation effort by Jess Campbell, an acquaintance who became his friend. The two often met each other in court and, more often, in Democratic Party meetings. McNalley and Campbell were some of the few Democrats that were members of Farragut Community Group—an admittedly nonpartisan organization.

But, as McNalley says, nothing is really nonpartisan.

And everything is political.

Take, for instance, Knoxville's annexation plans. There were a lot of people in Knox County who didn't want Knoxville to annex, to gain more tax revenue, to be an even bigger competitor for funds and resources. They, like McNalley, considered Farragut incorporating to be the lesser of two evils. And while that opinion may never have been made public, only a fool would believe it didn't help Farragut get started.

McNalley, sitting in Farragut's public library, grins mischievously. He's driven in from out of the area, unable to "afford even a lot in this town," he laughs. It's come a long way from the "Farragut Farmers," he says.

McNalley is cautious when he tells stories about the goings-on surrounding the incorporation, not wanting to implicate someone who helped Farragut when perhaps they shouldn't have, or anyone whose private stance was opposite from their public one. Or anyone who's still in elected office.

But it's clear that as far as McNalley's concerned, the Farragut incorporation was the exception to the normal rules.

"All contentious political things are decided beforehand. How many times have you ever seen an election certified immediately? How many times have you ever seen a city's charter certified in one day? Where was all the red tape?"

Some of that help may or may not have come from McNalley and Campbell themselves, especially considering the fact that the majority of election commissioners at the time also were Democrats. You'd never know for sure, though. McNalley will just smile when asked.

But he did a lot of things no one else in the Farragut Community Group knew about. After McGill was followed home, McNalley had a TBI friend of his stake out the McGill home for weeks, a fact McGill didn't learn until thirty years later. He called in favors to learn just how to put pressure on Knoxville Metropolitan Planning Commission members, which may or may not have resulted in the halting of the MPC's plans to zone all of Kingston Pike as commercial.

He may or may not have called a state representative he knew, who may or may not have helped move things through at the state level, perhaps resulting in the new town's charter being approved in mere minutes.

You just never know.

McNalley winks.

"You know, it'll be interesting to hear how other people remember things. Do you know what a police officer knows when he's interviewing two witnesses and they say the exact same thing? They're lying."

McNalley's memories aren't always the same as the other members of Farragut Community Group. But perhaps that's because he knew back-stories no one else did.

The Interstate Annexation

December 1979 — January 1980

Members of the Farragut Community Group would later say that Knoxville's own actions guaranteed Farragut's incorporation effort was successful.

Early in December, Knoxville Mayor Randy Tyree made a vow to halt the Farragut incorporation vote at any cost. He recruited Knoxville's law director, Jon Roach, to his cause, and set in motion the annexation study Betty Dick had heard about in early 1979. He told the newspapers he expected to have the annexation approved by Jan. 13, 1980, two days before the date that had been decided for the incorporation referendum.

"As state law presently is drafted, if a city like Knoxville passes an annexation ordinance, the area contemplating incorporation is precluded from doing so for 18 months," Tyree told *West Side Story*.

David and Ralph took a different tack.

The law Tyree was hoping would halt the referendum was the same law the incorporators had designed around when drawing up Farragut's borders. In certain situations, deference was given to a city that wished to annex before a smaller city could incorporate. If Farragut's borders were within five miles of Knoxville, the city would have had that option.

But they weren't.

And that was what Tyree was taking late action to change.

At a City Council meeting December 13, Tyree and Roach presented a plan to Knoxville's city council that annexed three miles of Interstate right-of-way. The annexation brought the city limits to within five miles of Farragut's proposed boundaries.

In the papers, Rodgers challenged Roach's and Tyree's reasoning, since state law also requires annexation to "mutually benefit" both the city and the residents in the area to be annexed. Rodgers said the city's actions wouldn't be legal, since no one lived on the Interstate and thus no one could benefit from being annexed into Knoxville.

Roach, when asked by Margaret Fifield of *The Oak-Ridger* who lived in the area that was to be annexed, said, "Well no one, really, unless you count the people going by in their cars."

Ralph and David attended the city council meeting to present the Farragut Community Group's arguments.

"If you vote to annex, you vote to steal the right of elective franchise from the people of Farragut just as if you voted to send armed, masked men in to steal the ballot box. You should vote against this ordinance because law and reason dictate it and justice and equity require it," David said, his voice ringing out in the city council chambers.

Only one city councilman voted against the ordinance.

His name was Arthur Blanchard, but he went by "Smiley."

During the meeting, he said, "I think it's unconstitutional, illegal and I'm not going to support it. It's a slap in the face of Farragut residents. They are fellow Knox Countians and council ought to show them the courtesy of doing their own thing."

After the successful vote, Ralph called the annexation "ludicrous and illegal."

The ordinance would go into effect two days before the referendum. That left the election commission in a lurch—did the annexation stop the referendum? Or, because the referendum had been scheduled first, did the annexation mean nothing?

"We're between the devil and the deep blue sea," election commission chair Gene Bell told *The News Sentinel*.

Bell took the dispute to court the very next day, asking the Chancery Court to rule whether Knoxville's actions prevented the referendum vote or not. A chancellor from the neighboring city of Morristown, William Inman, was called in as an impartial judge, and quickly decided Knoxville's ordinance wasn't active yet and thus wasn't preventing any referendum.

Bell announced that the referendum would be held as scheduled.

In January, Roach and Tyree were still on the offensive, declaring they would sue if Farragut were incorporated to ensure the new city didn't receive any federal funding.

"If they want to get it they must levy a tax. There's no free lunch," Tyree told *The Journal*.

Rodgers chuckled when the reporter asked him for his opinion on Tyree's comments. "That just goes to show how irresponsible they are at this point. That would be like Knoxville filing a suit against Nashville."

Jon Roach

Jon Roach remembers Farragut's incorporation as an "interesting time," laughing, years later, at the preparedness of Farragut Community Group members and especially of David Rodgers.

"David Rodgers was a very able attorney, very good attorney. And he thought of almost everything," Roach chuckles over the phone from his office on Gay Street in downtown Knoxville.

He's remembering the infamous Interstate finger annexation, the attempt to halt the incorporation by bringing Farragut's boundaries within five miles of Knoxville's.

"The existing city limits of the City of Knoxville were more than five miles from the proposed area that was to be incorporated by Farragut. Since we couldn't bring Farragut closer to Knoxville, we decided to bring Knoxville closer to Farragut," Roach laughed.

He also remembers taking a long look at the far west end of Farragut's proposed boundaries, noting a curious chunk of land off Watt Road left out—the land that was dropped because it was too close to Oak Ridge. That's the thought that prompts Roach's admiring comments about Rodgers.

Roach served as Knoxville's attorney from 1976 to 1983, when

Mayor Randy Tyree lost his reelection bid. He remained in Knoxville practicing law at Watson Roach Batson Rowell & Lauderback, his firm even representing Farragut in a lawsuit in later years.

Knoxville's finger annexations were becoming more common before Roach ever heard the words "Farragut Community Group," he remembers. A lawsuit over another attempted annexation of land in west Knox County had led to a 22-day court appearance, and after that 22-square mile attempt, Knoxville kept its annexations small. But Farragut's initial argument wasn't with Knoxville. It was with the County. Roach first heard of the incorporation effort in the newspapers.

"And then, among the Mayor and others in City government, the decision was made to try to prevent their incorporation," Roach said. "I think it was seen that Knoxville's growth had been and would be to the west, and we felt like if municipal services were needed in that area, then Knoxville was a more appropriate provider of those services."

The attempt to halt Farragut's incorporation with that Interstate annexation was a swing-and-a-miss because of timing, Roach remembers.

"The timing was such that we weren't able to get it dismissed before their election in April of 1980. And so ... time ran out before we could score. Once they had voted to incorporate, even though we won the lawsuit, they won the war."

The lawsuits were portrayed as confusing even in the newspapers— Knoxville's original suits named the Farragut Community Group members. Before the vote to incorporate in January, there was no reason to sue. After the incorporation was successful, the Group members weren't the right people to name in a lawsuit. By the time officials were elected in April, popular opinion called for Farragut's right to exist.

One thing Roach makes clear is his immense respect for David Rodgers.

"I first knew David when I was in law school. I clerked for a little over two years at the Kramer Rayson firm, and David was a young associate when I first went there to clerk. So I got to know him those years."

The dueling attorneys may have been on opposite sides in legal battles, but the pair weren't enemies. The two even sent each other comics, or "funnies," to one another over the years.

"I can't remember us ever having cross words with one another, even though we were opponents, or representing people opposed to one another. Sometimes it's hard to distinguish between the client and the attorney," Roach said.

"But David was always a gentleman. I always liked David."

The Last Meeting

January 10, 1980

Betty sat up straighter in her seat, leaning forward into the mic, her toes hitting the wire trailing from the table onto the floor and off the stage of the auditorium at Farragut High School. She cleared her throat.

"I am Betty Dick. My family and I live in Village Green," she began.

"Our area no longer has the choice of status quo; therefore, I believe the interest and energies of Farragut residents can best be served and utilized if we incorporate."

She read from a yellow legal pad; she'd written out her speech in pen, the pages scrawled with her slanted, looped writing and occasionally dotted with exclamation points in places where she couldn't keep her excitement off the page.

She related a few of her experiences with the Metropolitan Commission and couldn't stop herself from talking about the commissioner who hadn't let Ralph speak.

"A few months ago at a MPC meeting, the spokesman for our flood prevention committee was told by the MPC chairman who preceded Mrs. Stone, that our member did not have a legal right to speak—that the MPC did not have to listen to any speaker from the floor on any petition. Why do you suppose the chairman chose our speaker to resurrect the law on the books?"

"Ask yourself, why?" she stated, her temper flaring.

She went through several examples of the MPC's flawed decision making, but Betty didn't cite too many specifics, not wanting to bog down what needed to be a short, empowering speech.

"I do not mean to say that we in Farragut have been treated any differently than other areas, because we have not. MPC and CC members do not have to live out here with the problems—traffic, drainage, etc.—that they create. We do!" she said.

"We, in the community, can do a better job of planning, zoning and developing than either Knox County or Knoxville. Farragut can be a responsive and responsible decision-making government of the people. The only way to achieve this is to incorporate!" her voice rang out.

"Thank you," she said after a pause.

There was a smattering of applause around the room during the last meeting the Farragut Community Group held at the high school, the one they hoped would rally the final support for the referendum.

David stood up and answered a few questions about the lawsuit, but there weren't very many questions that remained unanswered for the voters in attendance at the rally. The newspapers were printing nearly daily stories about the incorporation effort, the annexation ordinance and the election commission. The details had been hashed and re-hashed in the papers. There wasn't much left to say.

So Jess Campbell took the opportunity to share his dreams.

"Incorporation will allow us to decide on our own government. We won't have to put up with developers who build in floodways," Jess began, looking down the stage to Ralph, who nodded. "We won't have to cringe every time we drive down roads that weren't built correctly to begin with," he said, thinking of roads like Campbell Station and Concord that were barely two lanes wide and were simply patch upon patch upon patch.

Jess looked out into the audience for Julie and George Dorsey, who had worked with him for so long on the Fox Den Homeowners' Association. "We won't have to make trips downtown in the hopes that our concerns will be heard," he said, watching the Dorseys clap in approval.

Jess sought out Eric in the crowd, smiling at him as he mentioned the next possibility: "We could prohibit the ugly signs that litter our streets and block our views." Eric's eyes sparkled as he laughed, picturing the real estate signs that blocked Peterson Road every week.

"We could have a tree preservation program. We could require shopping centers to have landscaped parking areas, rather than masses of asphalt," Jess said, gaining an approving murmur from the crowd of more than a hundred.

"We could require that roof lines hide air conditioning and heating units, and that developers have to screen trash containers, rather than having to look at them from the streets or from our homes," he added.

To the members of the Farragut Community Group, none of these ideas were significant only to Jess. They were shared. They weren't new or shocking or even earth-shattering.

But increasingly, they were possible.

"We'll be able to decide. Come out and vote," Jess proclaimed, his tall body leaning over the lectern.

The Scrambled Egg

January 1980

January 10, three days before Tyree's annexation would go into effect, David sued.

On behalf of the Farragut Community Group, Rodgers filed one suit in Chancery Court and another in Circuit Court against Knoxville, Tyree and each of the city councilmen, alleging they acted in violation of state laws with the Interstate annexation. The suits claimed the overriding intent of the annexation wasn't for annexation itself, but was in fact to delay an already-scheduled referendum.

The two suits named different plaintiffs, although all were members of Farragut Community Group or were supportive volunteers, and the suits asked that the defendants be required to appear in court to show why an injunction against their annexation not be issued.

David called it "the scrambled egg."

"Filing in two courts will further insulate the city from stopping the election," Rodgers told the *Journal*.

To the *Sentinel*, he said, "That way, the city can't unscramble the egg before the election. Even if the cases are dismissed, we have the right to appeal, which will further delay the effectiveness of the annexation until after the referendum."

"We're going to have an election."

Roach filed to dismiss the suits the next day, January 11, a Friday. He sought a hearing for Monday the 14th, the day before the referendum, as a last-ditch effort to stop the vote.

A judge didn't buy it.

At the Monday hearing, Chancellor Len Broughton clearly showed his frustrations. He had watched the suits exchanged between Knoxville and the Farragut Community Group for the past month, along with the rest of Knox County. And he was irritated the suits were being decided the day before the referendum, repeatedly taking off his glasses in court and glaring at the arguing attorneys.

"Lawsuits of this nature do nothing but cloud the issue for the electorate," he said, chastising the plaintiffs and defendants who sat before him. "This suit could have been filed sooner."

David, sitting at the bench, imagined the judge was disciplining children and did his best to hide a grin.

Broughton caught the smile, quickly demanding to know just why David had waited until January 10 to file a suit to stop an ordinance passed a month ago. David stood at the lectern to answer, not mincing words.

He said his clients, the Farragut Community Group, weren't prepared for a lawsuit in December, when the judge from out of town, Inman, had dismissed the suit that had been brought by the election commission. After the suit had been dismissed, he needed time to file another, he explained. David quickly made room for Roach to take the lectern when Broughton targeted him with the same question.

"We did not think we had standing until the effectiveness of the ordinance," Roach told him. David grimaced. The annexation had gone into effect the day before, Sunday.

But in the end, Broughton sided with the Farragut Community Group.

"The only people who will suffer if I halt the election are the people who put up their money and spent their time preparing for this election," he told Roach, narrowing his eyes and wiping his gleaming forehead.

"If the incorporation is not valid, regardless of the vote, this court can still protect the city," he continued, finally placing his glasses back upon the bridge of his nose and ending the hearing.

The vote would be held.

But the argument wasn't over.

Randy Tyree

For Randy Tyree, it all boiled down to timing.

Planning for the 1982 World's Fair was taking up most of his time; he was lobbying and traveling to Washington D.C. and beyond to plan what would be the last World's Fair widely regarded as successful. The New Orleans's Fair in 1984 would lose $110 million; Knoxville reportedly made $57 from its expo, which attracted more than 11 million people. Tyree would later say Knoxville invested about $45 million in both public and private funds and had a "$300 million return on investment." Tyree's Knoxville International Energy Exposition, backed by prominent businessmen Jake Butcher and Jim Haslam, was going to put his "scruffy little city" on the map.

And quite frankly, Farragut ranked pretty low on his list of priorities.

"On the cusp of the World's Fair, the issues that didn't have to be resolved just got put off," he says.

Tyree was Knoxville's mayor from 1976 to 1983, when he unsuccessfully ran for governor against incumbent Lamar Alexander. He never disappeared from politics completely, unsuccessfully running for Knox County sheriff in the mid-2000s. He was an attorney and continued practicing law in Knoxville when he wasn't running for office.

Tyree chuckles over the phone at the idea that Farragut's incorporators waited until he left town to file for a referendum in the election commission office.

"That sounds like my good friend David Rodgers," he says.

His interest in Farragut was precisely the same reason people in Farragut had no interest in Knoxville, he says: taxes. "The median income is higher in West Knoxville, particularly far West Knox County, so you had a lot of influential people there as well as a lot of financial interest in being able to pay only one tax rate, and that would be the Knox County property tax."

"It's like everything in government: follow the money," he adds.

That higher income was the reason most of Knoxville's finger annexations were to the west of the city limits, Tyree says. And he acknowledges annexations are divisive. But most of Knoxville's annexations were done by request of either residents or businesses—many of which desired the city's additional services even if it came at the cost of an additional tax.

The Interstate annexation was a notable exception, of course.

"If you annex Interstate, there's no one to object to it," Tyree says.

Knoxville's and Farragut's resultant lawsuits over that annexation languished in courts for a bit, Tyree remembers, simply because they didn't rank high enough to garner full attention. The World's Fair was held in 1982, a May-to-October extravaganza that left little room for anything else that year. By 1983, Tyree had moved on.

And in addition to all that, Tyree remembers, the county and the city had bigger governmental fish to fry. The Farragut incorporation fell between two unsuccessful attempts to consolidate governments—one vote in 1978 and the final vote in 1983. The two municipalities would eventually combine school systems, but the pair of governments considered each other bigger threats than either considered an incorporated Farragut.

While neither was exactly enthused with Farragut's incorporation, the two governments had very different reasons for opposing it—and perhaps different reasons for letting it slide.

Overall, Tyree has fond memories of Farragut's incorporation, even of the annexation battle and subsequent lawsuits, certainly of the people with whom he argued and even went to court.

"Everyone was always very gentlemanly, very scholarly. We didn't tell bad things about each other. It was a challenging but very telling time about how people with good will on all sides can come together and establish a success, even when there are many divergent opinions. That's my take on the overall situation," he says.

The Vote

January 15, 1980

It was a landslide victory.

More than 1,300 people came out to vote on the decision of incorporation: 1,020 voted in favor and 303 dissented.

The headlines reflected the three-to-one margin, captured the celebration of the Farragut Community Group and the unrelenting determination of the city of Knoxville and Randy Tyree, who continued undaunted with his efforts to negate the election.

"The ball game is still out there; this is just the preliminary event," Tyree told *Sentinel* writer Mike Cavender.

Paul Monger, a Fox Den resident, was the first to cast a vote in the incorporation referendum. He voted in December by absentee ballot, but because of special requirements for a referendum vote, had to vote in person at election commission offices downtown.

"The people should vote. They should exercise their rights," he told the *News-Sentinel*.

Rodgers and McGill's only disappointment was the number of people who turned out for the vote. The total turnout was only around half of the actual number of registered voters in Farragut, about 2,700, and only a fraction of the total population—6,000.

"I feel great. I expected this size margin, but I expected a larger turnout," Rodgers told the *Sentinel*.

Larry Vaughn echoed those thoughts. "My only disappointment is the number of people who did not turn out; that they did not feel it affected them enough to turn out." He quickly assured reporters there were no hard feelings, as far as he was concerned, about the voting results.

"I'll not move away because of the outcome. I hope it works," the *Sentinel* reported Vaughn saying.

Rodgers' only other quote for the paper concerned Tyree's promise to continue fighting the incorporation: "I think my legal position is sound and correct. I think we'll prevail in our position."

He was positive the City was in the wrong—the incorporation papers had been filed long before Tyree went forward with his Interstate annexation and Farragut's boundaries had been outside the five-mile mark. The incorporation should stand. They'd followed all the rules, had made middle-of-the-night runs to correct their boundary mistake on the Oak Ridge side.

There'd be no going back now because of the City's Hail Mary annexation.

Tyree, for his part, had no shortage of things to say to the papers.

He and Roach promised to continue their suit with Broughton, to determine just how the Interstate annexation would affect the referendum vote, now that they knew the vote itself was successful.

"The question now is at what point does the statute take place," Tyree said of the state law. "If that holds, the election is a moot point. If it doesn't, the residents have a new city."

And if the Farragut incorporation did stand, Tyree had plenty to say about that too.

"If they want revenue sharing funds, they must set a tax rate. There are no free lunches. We'll file suit to stop them. We'll take whatever means are necessary to protect Knoxville's interest. If they want revenue sharing, they must do like everybody else and pay taxes to get it. They said they wouldn't set a tax rate. Revenue sharing comes from local taxes. Federal revenue sharing laws give priority to municipalities that have a tax rate," he said.

The Group members celebrated the successful vote at The Longbranch restaurant, along with referendum and incorporation volunteers, friends and family. Even members of the media were invited, including Margaret Fifield, who wrote about the party in *The Oak Ridger*.

Marianne McGill led the entire group in an impromptu and improvisational version of "Rocky Top," with "Good ole Farragut; Farragut, Tennessee," substituted in for the chorus of the boisterous game song chanted at University of Tennessee football games. Signs were hung all over the restaurant proclaiming, "You can fight city hall," "We did it," and "V for victory." There was some talk and planning about the city vote to elect Farragut's first mayor and aldermen, which election commissioners had planned for April 1.

Rodgers took issue with that date, hoping the election could have been held sooner. He did not want to leave Farragut without a government for months while the town would simultaneously be fighting lawsuits from the city of Knoxville.

But through the newspapers, election commissioner Richard Krieg told him, "You had an opportunity to elect your mayor and aldermen today. I have no sympathy for you."

Rodgers and other members of Farragut Community Group had deliberately opted not to have the vote for elected officials at the same referendum that would create the town, trying to avoid confusion or even a possible split vote. No one wanted to risk the town being voted down simply because the candidates for elected officials weren't who someone wanted.

Krieg and the other commissioners ultimately explained an entirely new voter list would have to be created before any vote could be taken on elected officials. Since the Town now was its own entity, it needed its own voter list. After that explanation, Rodgers dropped his argument.

Instead, he began gearing up for the continued fight against the city of Knoxville.

Others, even among the celebrators, started their own plans to run for aldermen and mayoral positions. Eric Johnson's wife, Jan, would turn in her name for mayor, and so would Bill Etter. Eric would do the same for alderman, as would George Dorsey, Marianne McGill and Dewey Young.

The celebration continued, eventually ending at the Johnsons' the next morning.

George Dorsey

George Dorsey never wanted to be involved.

His wife, Julie, was the community activist. He was a chemist. But somehow, she talked him into serving the remainder of her stint on the Board of the Fox Den homeowners association.

That's where he got to know Jess Campbell. That's how he heard about the idea of incorporating.

The incorporators first got out maps and began marking future town boundaries on the Dorseys' living room floor.

"The more I got involved, the more I understood. The area was just growing rapidly, too rapidly without controls. If there was a plan, no one was following it. And there should have been a plan. It was pretty obvious what we needed to do. We just needed to do it," he says. Dorsey's voice is quiet, measured. He's a scientist; trained to calculate and weigh options and choose the most logical.

Dorsey spends a lot of time explaining just why he chose to join the Farragut Community Group; perhaps he's explaining it to himself. He and the others make many references to being "thirty-something and too stupid to know any better." Even to them, even when incorporating became their best or only option, it did not always seem to be the most logical choice. To a group of scientific-minded men and women, just how they ended up becoming involved in an incorporation effort still seems to be a mystery.

"The more we studied it, the more we realized this was doable. We'd be stupid not to do it," Dorsey says, sitting at his dining room table. He and Julie still live in the same home they've lived in since moving to Farragut in 1973.

While the incorporators had hoped for, and even partially expected, a successful incorporation vote, no one expected the vote to be such a landslide.

"It was very hard to ignore Knoxville's annexation," Dorsey says, smirking. His eyes twinkle under his shock of white hair.

The Farragut Community Group members still laugh, years after the incorporation, at the city's hasty move. They widely acknowledge that the incorporation vote might not have been quite the rout it was if Knoxville hadn't pushed the envelope with the Interstate annexation.

Dorsey leans back into the dining room chair and chuckles again.

The day after the election, Dorsey volunteered to drive Farragut's charter to Nashville, accompanied by David Rodgers. Wanting the most reliable ride, they took Dorsey's new car, a 1979 diesel station wagon, too excited to chat much on the four-hour or so trip to the state capital. Dorsey imagined walking into an opulent office, sitting down and waiting while paperwork was filed and facts were checked, while a signature and a seal were painstakingly applied.

Instead, the pair walked into a ground-floor office painted that familiar municipal beige, and straight up to a counter where a woman stood waiting. She smiled as Rodgers introduced himself, waving a man at the desk behind her to get a pen and the seal. The man returned and certified the charter. The whole process took maybe ten minutes.

Dorsey strongly suspected someone—most likely Jess or Gene, who both had so many friends—had greased the skids. It was certainly no coincidence that the election results were certified the same day of the election and that the next morning, only a little more than twelve hours later, the state certified Farragut's charter. But Dorsey and Rodgers were too excited to give it much thought. Dorsey took his cheap slim-line camera out of his pocket and photographed David at the counter with the charter, and asked someone outside the capital to take a picture of the pair of them. Then they sped home to share the good news: Farragut existed, at least in the state's eyes.

That night, they returned to the Farragut Community Group members, continuing the celebration. They also began laying out, more formally, their plans on just who should run for election in April.

The Group was determined to have a contingent of members run for aldermen or mayoral positions, to ensure that no one was elected who then might move to take the Town in a direction the Group didn't want, or to dissolve it entirely.

George leans back in the chair at the head of his dining room table, remembering that Jess Campbell convinced him to run. He is modest about his own contributions to the Group, how he was the de facto leader for months before McGill joined the group. Dorsey doesn't talk willingly about just why someone would want him to run for alderman. But it's no leap to see why Jess asked him to run—because of that modesty, because of that tendency to weigh every option carefully.

And in the early years of the town, when elected officials faced lawsuits from the city, from developers and even from its own citizens, George remembers being thankful for his even keel, his ability to listen to lengthy exposés from attorneys and only ask for clarification, to not get involved in arguments and criticisms.

So George—who never intended to get involved in politics at all— ran for alderman.

The Lawsuits

After the incorporation, Farragut Community Group members continued the fight against the city's Interstate annexation and subsequent lawsuits.

Only three days after the referendum, Chancellor Broughton dealt a blow to their hopes when he dismissed one of the suits the Group had filed against the city. Broughton ruled the citizens who sued the city—the Group members—didn't own property in the annexed area and couldn't be classified as aggrieved parties. Therefore, their suit had no standing.

"At this point we do not know what ultimate effect this will have on incorporation. We will seek a conference with Chancellor Broughton to clarify this," David Rodgers told the *News-Sentinel*. "I know of no adverse effect, however, that this has on incorporation. The city of Farragut exists. It has to proceed with election of officials April 1. It has its charter from the secretary of state."

Newspapers broke down the ruling in article after article, headlines proclaiming the dismissal created confusion.

The confusion didn't last long.

February 1, Broughton dismissed the city's suit to halt incorporation on the grounds that the city didn't have anyone to sue. Broughton ruled that because Farragut had, in fact, incorporated successfully through the referendum vote, city law director Jon Roach's suit wasn't directed against the correct people. A lawsuit from Roach would have to be directed to Farragut elected officials; and as of yet, there were none.

"You are asking me to make a ruling which would be binding on no one," Broughton told Roach in court.

Roach promised to bring the suit back once Farragut had officials to sue.

Eric Johnson and Ralph McGill appealed Broughton's dismissal of their suit against the city. By September, it was heard by the state Supreme Court, who affirmed the Chancery Court's dismissal. The Supreme Court also refused to consider the city's contention that the annexation became effective before the referendum and therefore negated Farragut's incorporation.

"I honestly don't know what it means," David said of the various dismissals.

"I'll have to look at it. What I think it is saying is, 'If you want to do anything else, you'll have to take another shot at it. You'll have to file another lawsuit,'" he added.

Ultimately, the incorporation stood—but Farragut's legal battles were far from over.

After Farragut's first election for the Board of Mayor and Aldermen, Tyree announced plans to annex down Kingston Pike to Concord Road, literally coming to Farragut's doorstep. The move would have added 42,000 people to Knoxville's limits. Farragut's Board drafted a resolution asking the city to annex "only the populated areas logically associated with their city," and to consider subdivisions such as Lovell View, Concord Hills and Thornton Heights as part of the Farragut community, as they always had been.

At the same time Tyree announced his annexation plans, Farragut was facing its third request from local subdivisions to annex. By May, the Board had approved annexation of Sweetbriar subdivision and Woodland Trace subdivision, both of which had already been approved for annexation by Knoxville. The subdivisions had asked to be annexed into Farragut. State law gave Knoxville the preference to annex first, within 180 days. Knoxville didn't make that move and the more than twenty-square-mile annexation ultimately was unsuccessful. Knoxville eventually took the tack of annexing smaller bits of land at a time.

But the city wasn't the town's only opponent in court.

In the months after the April election, Farragut elected officials also sued Knox County in Chancery Court for the Town's portion of state sales tax revenue, which the county was withholding. The county's argument for holding the funds was that all of its state-shared sales tax revenue went to schools. Rodgers conceded that half of Farragut's sales tax revenue—an amount required by the state—would go to operate schools, but the other half would go into the town's general fund.

In July 1980, Knox County Chancery Court sided with Farragut, ruling the money had to be made available each month to the town. The entire amount of money due to the town, since incorporation in January, reached about $25,000. The county also was told it had no standing to contest beer tax funds the town had been receiving that the county allocated to fund public libraries.

In the end, Farragut received those funds as well.

PART III
A New Government

The Election

April 1980

It was a twenty-candidate field.

In the running were engineers, attorneys, a psychologist, a sociologist and a surgical nurse. Headlines proclaimed the "brainpower" of the "skilled elite" that could provide initial leadership in Farragut.

Mayoral candidates included Bill Etter, who composed the budget for the town before it ever existed, and who was proclaimed a "kingpin in the Farragut incorporation movement" by the *Knoxville Journal*. Jan Johnson, Eric Johnson's wife, was initially listed in the running, but Eric was running unopposed for a one-year seat in the south ward. Jan withdrew because of the possible conflict of interest.

She encouraged Bob Leonard to withdraw as well, citing his job as First Utility District's attorney as a similar clash. Leonard denied the conflict.

Also in the running was Ted Lundy, the county squire who had held the voter registration book during the incorporation process, and Bill Shipley, a critic of incorporation and member of the Concerned Citizens Committee. Lundy also held a Ph.D. in metallurgical engineering and worked at Oak Ridge National Laboratory. He was largely considered the most likely to win, since he was the most experienced politician and had the most name recognition. But without a doubt, Leonard generated the most public interest … and the most controversy.

Bill Etter, like Johnson, called on Leonard to step down from the race because of the possibility of conflict, in instances such as First Utility District deciding to proceed with condemnation suits in the town. Leonard called Etter's campaign negative, and said if his position with First Utility ever became a conflict, he'd simply recuse himself.

"His charges will hurt him more than they will hurt me," he told the *Journal.*

In addition to Eric Johnson's unopposed run for alderman in the south ward, George Dorsey, Margie Cramer and Winston Kegley ran for the one-year term in the north ward. Cramer was a surgical nurse; Kegley was a planning engineer for South Central Bell.

Running for a two-year term in the north ward were K. Wynne James III, a tax attorney who raised eyebrows for his advocacy of a property tax, and Marianne McGill.

James was quoted in the *Journal* as saying, "I think that the expectations that the city will have a surplus without a property tax are unrealistic and utopian. In the face of decreased sales tax collections, revenue sharing cuts and high inflation, I find it very difficult to believe that the city of Farragut can operate without a small property tax."

Also running against McGill and James were Gene Brady, a salesman at Union Carbide, and Harold McReynolds, a sales representative. Brady's platform largely involved "keeping out undesirable adult entertainment districts that threaten to move into the area," according to the *Journal.*

Finally, in the running for the south ward's two-year term were Eddy Ford, a nuclear engineer at Union Carbide; Gerald Kirk Eddlemon, a research associate at ORNL; Jack Coleman, a psychologist; Larry Feezel, a social worker; and Dewey Young, the civil engineer at Union Carbide that Eric Johnson had dubbed "Mr. Magoo."

Ford told the *Journal* he wanted a "no frills government" and opposed "commercial clutter." He owned a large parcel of land in the center of Farragut and acknowledged that most who moved to the town came to escape urban problems and thus, the community should work to prevent "the spread of undesirable development." Ford also advocated volunteerism as the best method to cut costs in the fledgling government while still getting things done.

All of the elected officials would be volunteers; none would collect a salary.

The election was held April 1, and 1,233 people came out to vote—about one-third of the total registered voters in the town. News stories called the turnout "poor by most standards," although a *News-Sentinel* story noted many people in the area were on spring vacations.

Leonard, despite—or perhaps because of—the controversy surrounding his position as First Utility District's attorney, was elected mayor handily with 555 total votes, beating Bill Etter by 107 votes and Ted Lundy by 353 votes. Shipley and Jan Johnson together received twenty-eight votes, although both had withdrawn from the race by election day.

Etter expressed his displeasure in a *Journal* piece written by Robert Jones: "I don't want to sound like sour grapes, but Leonard is backed by special interests and he spent a lot of money on this campaign."

Marianne McGill won her race by seventy-nine votes. Ford and Dorsey won by more than 100 votes each. Eric Johnson, of course, was elected unopposed.

An article in the *Journal* questioned Leonard's standing on a Board composed of three members of the Farragut Community Group, particularly considering Johnson and McGill both had come out against Leonard during the election, citing his position with First Utility as a conflict of interest.

But during a celebration at his home the Tuesday night of the election, Leonard dismissed those problems to *Journal* reporter Jones. "This council must put behind it what has gone before. As a candidate I offered to bridge the gap between the opposition."

Leonard next made news for his courtesy visit to Randy Tyree.

A *News-Sentinel* editorial quoted him as saying, "the two cities don't necessarily need to be adversaries," that Farragut "was not looking for any fights. But if we have them, we'll deal with them when they come. That's said in the spirit of Adm. Farragut, though not as forceful as when he stood on the deck of his flagship, the Hartford, while it inched its way through a minefield during the battle of Mobile Bay, and told the other Union ships: 'Damn the torpedoes, full speed ahead!'"

Bob Leonard

Bob Leonard has a voice that belies his stature.

The small, thin man sits in his home office, behind a table he says his children grew up eating around. As he reminisces, his voice echoes around the small room, perhaps a learned vocal trait from his years as an attorney.

Leonard and his wife, Marie, are well-known features around Farragut, still living in the Village Green home they moved to in 1971. He was the Town's first mayor, serving for six terms. He remembers hearing about the incorporation idea and deciding he'd run for the office.

"I bought into it hook, line and sinker. I thought it was splendid," Bob said, although others remember him expressing displeasure with incorporation in its early stages.

Whether he agreed with incorporating or not, it is clear Leonard is proud of his time as mayor, showing off a plaque naming him Tennessee Municipal League Mayor of the Year, autographed originals of political cartoons about Farragut, and framed letters from other government officials congratulating him on his retirement in 1993.

It's also clear he considered himself the best man for the job of mayor.

"None of the other people running had any government experience except being greatly disappointed with County Court. I knew every person of any stature at the Knox County Court House. I knew all the people the founders didn't."

Those connections were partially the reason members of Farragut Community Group opposed him, a fact he recognizes.

"They thought I was too connected." Bob was the long-time attorney of First Utility District, a fact Group members considered a conflict of interest. But he says his connections provided Farragut a start it never would have had otherwise. And that's probably true.

Leonard is the man who negotiated Farragut's urban growth boundaries with Knox County and the city of Knoxville, drawing out where Farragut could expand without argument from either of the other municipalities, putting an end to years of lawsuits after the Town had incorporated.

Leonard remembers being the one who insisted on building Town Hall, on operating with as little debt as possible, on constructing parks in every quadrant of the Town, on having pedestrian sidewalks and bike paths throughout Farragut and for having the idea of beginning the Farragut Folklife Museum—perhaps partially inspired by the World's Fair Folklife Festival celebrating Appalachian culture.

And it's no secret Bob insists on having his way.

In fact, that was one of the first big fights between Farragut's first elected Board of Mayor and Aldermen. The Board wanted to jointly appoint members of Farragut's planning commission, saying Leonard was a "weak mayor" in the Board of Mayor and Aldermen system. Leonard resisted, citing state law that puts that responsibility of making appointments solely in the hands of the mayor. In the end, he allowed each alderman to suggest names for consideration, and Bob, as mayor, had the final pick.

He prides himself on that compromise, and on dozens of others.

And mostly he prides himself on how he helped set up Farragut to operate. "From the beginning, it was our intention to live off state shared sales tax ... and hopefully never impose a property tax. It makes Farragut a tax haven, if you will, and that was our intention."

"I always wanted the town of Farragut to be beautiful, green, with parks for children. We're heavy on amenities that benefit the whole community."

One thing Bob does not consider himself to be is a politician. Mayor, yes. Attorney, certainly. Peacemaker, dealmaker; yes. "I'm not really a politician, but winning six times—I guess that makes me a politician," he says of his many years of service as mayor.

Because of term limits enacted in 2010, the distinction of being elected to six terms as mayor will forever be distinct to Leonard.

Also distinct to Leonard is being the first to be elected to what would be Knox County's second mayoral office. At the time, only Knoxville had a mayor; the County had an "executive." Farragut was the County's third municipality, but the municipality was second to have a mayor. Years later, in fact, Randy Tyree would remember Leonard joking with him about it: "You don't want Farragut to succeed because then you'll only be second-best mayor," Bob had told him.

Bob leans back in his chair, smiling, recalling that he voluntarily decided not to run for a seventh term. The job was simply too consuming. "Your life is not really your own," he said, gesturing out of the room and down the hallway, where Marie is in the kitchen. The couple had three children, and Leonard wanted to spend more time with them. But Bob never disappeared from the Farragut scene, even later representing various homeowners and developers who had problems with Farragut regulations.

For Farragut's first mayor, the town has lived up to every potential he saw: a simple vision, in the end.

"We would have a careful, small government. And that's what we did."

Eddy Ford

Eddy Ford and his wife, Linda, were both raised in the Farragut area. They were the last couple to be married in their church, Concord United Methodist, before the church moved out of the historical village of Concord and toward the commercially developing Kingston Pike.

"The community was entirely different then," Eddy remembers from his living room, a two-story brick home situated on rolling acreage at the center of Farragut, near the home he was raised in. He recalls the time when there was only one traffic light in town at the intersection of Concord Road and Kingston Pike.

He doesn't remember when he first heard about incorporation, outside of reading it in the newspapers. "It was just general knowledge," he says. And running for elected office wasn't something that initially interested him—until a friend, Larry Patrick, asked him to run. As Ford says, the Farragut Community Group had already placed candidates in the race, and the fear among local landowners and long-time residents was that no one would run against them.

That turned out not to be a problem in Ford's particular race: he ran against four other men, including the Farragut Community Group's Dewey Young. "I went door-to-door and raised $70 in campaign contributions," Eddy says, chuckling at the amount.

It was while visiting neighbors door-to-door that Ford met Bob Leonard at his home in Village Green. Leonard was wearing a suit on a Saturday, an oddity, and a memory that's stuck with Eddy for more than thirty years.

"You don't see many people in a suit at home on Saturday," he laughs. Ford and Leonard would become political allies, and Eddy would later succeed his older colleague as mayor when Bob stepped down in 1993. That's not to say the two never disagreed.

In fact, there was no lack of disagreements among the first Board of Mayor and Aldermen. The group was a force of strong personalities and determined ideas of what the new town should be like.

"That's putting it politely," Eddy says with a wry smile.

The Board butted heads over contentious items as varied as who should appoint members to Farragut's planning commission to definitions for Farragut sign ordinances, from how to handle lawsuits from developers and residents to whether to fund Knox County's public library system. Ford was often the lone dissenting vote on contentious issues, and was the only member of the Board that avoided being personally named in a lawsuit from a local developer.

The developer's name was Culan Biddle, and he owned property that he wished to develop with a K-Mart. The problem he had was that his plans had been approved by Knox County before the Town was created, but because he hadn't begun actual construction, Biddle had to rework his plans to comply with Farragut's new rules. In the end, he sued Johnson, Dorsey, McGill and Leonard for $1 million apiece. Ford wasn't named. When asked why he thinks he wasn't included in the suit, Ford shrugs and says Biddle and his attorney, Keith McCord, must have considered Ford's requests to be more reasonable than the others'.

It's clear that this is a definition Ford prides himself upon— being the reasonable politician. He recalls being the lone dissenting vote in a decision that the Town would pay David Rodgers for work he performed for the Farragut Community Group, before the town technically existed. He also was the only dissenting vote when Knox County requested Farragut contribute payments for the public library system. The town ultimately paid $37,000 to the system, "a lot of money for a town our size." Ford had made a motion to pay on a per capita basis, which would have amounted to significantly less money.

Despite personality differences and divided votes, that first Board approved a host of ordinances that covered basic needs, including zoning plans and signage requirements. "They were basic ordinances for a town to function, a town oriented toward residents," Eddy says.

But what Ford remembers most proudly were the town's first hires—recorder Mary Lou Koepp and administrator Jack Hamlett—as well as Farragut's copious volunteers, men like Eddy's friend Bill Maney or Doug Wiley, who owned a tractor and mowed Town property before Farragut could afford public works crews.

But he is most enthusiastic about Koepp, the Town's very first employee: "That was the best hire this town has ever made." His wife, Linda, was on the committee that hired Koepp. She worked on an IBM Selectric typewriter with a small copy machine, switching from Millie McBride's word-for-word meeting minutes to action minutes.

"She did a tremendous job," Ford says.

Ford largely stepped away from political life and community activism after losing a mayoral election in 2009 to Ralph McGill in a landslide. He's not apt to giving long speeches, kind words or fond remembrances for all of his time with the town, but it's clear Ford is proud of his accomplishments as alderman and later, as mayor. Perhaps he recalls more of the dissension than other members of that first Board, but perhaps that's because he often was the dissenter.

In any case, Ford holds the record for longest-serving political official in the town, a record no one will ever top because of term limits—he served in one position or another, continuously, from 1980 to 2009, a total of 29 years.

And Ford has generous parting words regarding the personalities employed by and serving the town in 1980.

"For the most part, these people got along well together."

The Board

April 7, 1980

For the past four months, the Town of Farragut had only existed as paperwork kept in David Rodgers' briefcase.

Everything from lawsuits to town funding had stalled in the absence of elected officials, or even a Town employee. Until this night, there weren't any. But on Monday, April 7, nearly a hundred people gathered at Farragut High School at 8:00 to see Farragut's new elected officials— Bob Leonard, Eddy Ford, Eric Johnson, Marianne McGill and George Dorsey—sworn in.

Lamar Orr was the master of ceremonies. He was the president of First Utility District, as well as head of the science department at Farragut High School. The High School band played "The Star-Spangled Banner" after Cub Scout Den No. 2 led the Pledge of Allegiance.

Each of the new aldermen and the mayor were introduced, walking out onto the stage as if at an awards ceremony. This was the culmination of all of the hard work of the Farragut Community Group and the end of the stall-out following the incorporation vote: when the town existed but had no real substance. Judge Joe Duncan from the Knox County Court of Criminal Appeals administered the oath of office to each official.

The entire ceremony, including a brief speech from Leonard, lasted a total of twenty-one minutes.

"I must remind you, there will be no easy solutions to the problems that come before us," Leonard told the crowd of about 100. "The responsibilities to be faced by your town council are immense, but with your help, your support and your cooperation, we will not fail. You must also sacrifice your comfort and ease. You, too, must give of your time and of your effort. There will be a great need for citizen advisory groups in the operation of our town that go beyond concerns over zoning and planning."

"Optimism and enthusiasm are in the very air. United in a spirit of harmony and cooperation, I know that we can press on and achieve the results desired by us all. Our community wanted and wants a government small enough to know you and big enough to serve you. But no bigger," Leonard said.

After the swearing in ceremony, Leonard immediately called the first Board of Mayor and Aldermen meeting to order.

Now the work began.

The first order of business was hiring a town recorder; the Board immediately designated Millie McBride as recorder for the next sixty days. McBride had helped the Farragut Community Group put together the voter book and had already been keeping the minutes of the installation ceremony. Immediately after naming McBride temporary recorder, the Board named David Rodgers as the town attorney.

The third order of business was slightly trickier, but still passed without discussion except by Rodgers: the Board voted to annex Farragut Intermediate School and Farragut Middle School, which had been too close to Knoxville's borders to be included in the original incorporation boundaries, but had always been in the Farragut Community Group's sights as part of the town. After all, the town had taken the name of the schools, the name the community had become identifiable with. FCG members considered it understood that all of the schools that had lent their names to the Town would be officially part of it.

At the end of the meeting, Bill Touchstone presented the Board with a petition to annex land just outside Town limits, land that included the Sweetbriar and Woodland Trace subdivisions, as well as some land along Campbell Station Road. The Board agreed to put the annexation into proper format and discuss it at one of its work sessions, which were planned for every Monday and Thursday. Most of them would take place at First Utility District's offices.

Leonard also made a pronouncement that would come to be the Board's first—and perhaps most vocal—disagreement: that the Town would use the services of the Knoxville Knox County Metropolitan Planning Commission, rather than forming its own.

Marianne McGill took almost immediate issue with the idea, then with the idea that if the Town did form its own planning commission, that Leonard would have the authority under state law to appoint every member unilaterally.

At its next few meetings, though, it became more and more apparent that the Board needed to quickly come up with a solution to the planning commission debacle. Citizen requests flowed in, covering everything from building permits to complaints about children riding horses down subdivision streets and leaving piles of manure on the pavement.

"If we don't adopt something, we are setting the stage for the rape of this community up and down Kingston Pike," Leonard said at the Board's second meeting, perhaps a bit theatrically. He advocated that Metropolitan Planning Commission zoning already in place at the time of incorporation be adopted as an interim zoning, until the Board could rewrite its own.

By the Board's third meeting, they'd drafted an ordinance that would create a nine-member zoning board consisting of the mayor, one alderman chosen by the Board and seven citizens chosen by the mayor.

That idea again drew criticism from Marianne, who drafted a resolution calling on Leonard to choose from a list of candidates approved by the Board.

"I will not bind myself to choose from a group of people when the law does not require that. It is a bad precedent. I view it as an attack upon the powers of mayor," Leonard told her.

Marianne responded that she was merely trying to make the process more democratic.

"I view this as an attempt to circumvent the clear mandate of the law. Some people in the community will view it as a lack of faith in the mayor. Some will think there is a division on the board. I have asked you all to submit names for this process. Your names will probably be many of those I'm thinking of, because we know so many of the same people. I have no axe to grind. This is not an appropriate resolution," Leonard said.

In the end, Leonard won his argument.

He did take recommendations from the Board, but refused to bind himself to the option of choosing only from those names.

And he didn't make any decision without attracting more criticism.

Bill Sonnenthal, an incorporation advocate who attended the Board meeting at which the Farragut planning commissioners were named, said, "When I voted for incorporation, I had no idea of putting zoning in the hands of one man and his hand-picked cronies. Hell, we might as well be part of Knoxville."

By the middle of May, Leonard had named his seven appointees to Farragut's newly formed planning commission. Six were, after all, nominees of the Board: Michael Carle, Tom McFee, Tom Slawson, Jeff Klopatek, Charles McMurray, Connie Rutenber and Larry Patrick. The Board named Marianne McGill as its alderman representative, and Leonard rounded out the commission.

The men and women picked had different backgrounds and points-of-view. Rutenber had helped Farragut Community Group with the voter registration book. Tom Slawson and Jeff Klopatek also had been members of the Group. Tom McFee and Larry Patrick were long-time residents of Farragut. McFee was a prominent landowner.

But Klopatek perhaps garnered the most recognition—both at the time and when remembered by others, thirty years later. He worked at ORNL with many Farragut Community Group members, had a Ph.D. and worked as a research ecologist. He was named chair of the planning commission and, although he ultimately only served for little more than a year, many members of the first Board of Mayor and Aldermen acknowledged his work as instrumental in getting Farragut off the ground. Everyone on all sides of that particular controversy remember Klopatek as being the best man for the planning commission job.

Klopatek moved out of state in July 1981, but not before he and the FMPC adopted a 100-page zoning ordinance, zoning map and land use plan.

Leonard remembers his part in the FMPC controversy as solving what seemed an insurmountable problem, right out of the gate, with a compromise that still left the best people for the commission in place.

For his appointments, Leonard received a standing ovation from the twenty-or-so-member audience to the Board of Mayor and Aldermen meeting.

The School Tax

Spring to Fall, 1980

Some Farragut founders would tell you that people in Knox County positions of authority gave Farragut behind-the-scenes help during its incorporation effort, considering a new, small municipality to be a safer choice than a larger, more powerful Knoxville.

And that very well could be fact.

But that didn't mean the county was exactly happy when the incorporation effort turned out to be successful. In fact, the county became one of Farragut's primary opponents during the town's first year of existence, after the county trustee refused to release state-shared sales tax revenue that technically belonged to Farragut. The money the Town should have received over about a year's time was estimated at $105,000.

So David Rodgers sued.

"On Tuesday, April 22, 1980, the Mayor of Farragut was informed by Knox County Judge C. Howard Bozeman that no disbursement of [local option sales tax] funds would be made by the Knox County Trustee to the City of Farragut," stated the lawsuit, filed in the county's Chancery Court April 29. Rodgers named the county, Bozeman and county trustee Robert Broome as defendants.

"There is deposited with the Knox County Trustee the sum of $16,188.97," that belongs to the Town, the suit alleged. Half of that money was to be dedicated, according to state law, to the county for school purposes. The rest was supposed to go to Farragut.

The county historically gave all—rather than just half—of its local option sales tax money to the schools, and refused to release funds to Farragut on the grounds that the town should do the same.

After a hearing in July, the Chancery Court backed Farragut.

"The Town of Farragut is entitled to have disbursed to it ... one-half of the total local option sales tax collected within the geographical boundaries of the Town of Farragut. ... Future sales tax disbursements to the Knox County Trustee by the Tennessee Department of revenue for and on behalf of the Town of Farragut shall be disbursed in accordance with this Judgment," the judgment, filed August 4, stated.

The county appealed the ruling to the state court of appeals.

And in the meantime, county officials declared that without 100 percent of Farragut's local option sales tax going to schools, they would no longer improve any schools located in Farragut.

By November, Bob Leonard had seen enough.

"The Board of Mayor and Aldermen of the Town of Farragut has never taken an adversary position to the interests of its school children and of all the school children of West Knox County, nor does it do so now," he wrote in a letter dated November 13, 1980, that apparently was distributed to area residents.

Leonard said he'd tried to negotiate a solution with county and school officials, but had been met with, at best, unhelpful behavior. He asked school superintendent Earl Hoffmeister for the percentage of students who attended schools that bore the name "Farragut" who actually lived in town limits.

It turned out to be just around forty percent at Farragut Intermediate and Middle. It was somewhat higher at the Primary School, much less at the High School, Leonard said. As far as Leonard and the Board saw, Farragut shouldn't be solely financially responsible for schools where "60 percent of the children directly affected do not live in the Town of Farragut."

In addition, Bob argued that the county might be losing local option sales tax, but it was saving money elsewhere—the county was no longer responsible for any street maintenance in Farragut, the metropolitan planning commission no longer served Farragut residents and the county refused to share services of its hydrologist.

"All of these factors must be considered and government should always look at both sides of the coin before making a decision," Leonard said.

Later in the year, the state court upheld the county chancery court's decision.

Farragut received its funds.

David Rodgers called the victory "substantial," keeping true to his normal even-keel personality.

In a 1981 *News-Sentinel* article, Rodgers said, "This was a judicial recognition of the existence of the town. The availability of sales tax monies to a town is one of the critical planks in the scheme of municipal finance. This decision establishes the right to future sales taxes as the town grows."

Although Farragut did receive its sales tax money, and in fact continues to operate on a budget comprised largely of sales tax, the school funding controversy is still remembered by Knox County residents. Many still consider Farragut as getting a "free ride" in regards to school funding, as Farragut keeps its half of the local option sales tax and as Town residents don't pay a separate Farragut property tax.

Knox County does maintain Farragut schools.

The Long Nights

Summer 1980

Each ordinance had to be read aloud one at a time.

Every regulation and rule of the new Town, every by-law, every single written guideline, had to be read aloud individually for its first reading and recorded into the minutes of each meeting.

And that meant every meeting for that first year the Board met was very, very long.

"And that's not taking into account the fact that we have to argue over every single little thing," Marianne told Ralph the morning after a particularly long meeting. "Or that we have to listen to Eddy as he goes into each document and finds every spelling error or typo or miscalculation," she continued.

At the meetings, Bob, Marianne, Eric and George would take turns reading aloud while Eddy listened and proofread, calling out changes after it had all been read.

"Someone needs to be looking at that," Ralph conceded. "It's frustrating and time-consuming, but the town doesn't need to take chances and adopt an ordinance that is incorrect, even if it's only a technical error."

Marianne sighed.

"It's not upsetting that he does it. It's just upsetting that I have to sit through it," she laughed.

The Board had established committees to help write the ordinances, but each elected official was pulling their weight as well. Betty wrote the sign ordinance with the help of another Village Green resident, Carol Evans, who had been appointed to the Visual Resources Review Board. The pair and their respective families traveled to cities around the southeast, taking photographs of signs they liked, of cities that looked orderly and clean. They also traveled to and copied ordinances from cities like Brentwood and Germantown with Municipal Technical Advisory Service representative Ron Martin, tailoring those to Farragut.

"I'm not having it look like Kingston Pike further down … or like Chapman Highway," Betty would say to Jeremy as she traipsed along with camera in hand in Florida, South Carolina, Georgia, wherever they were—ignoring the scenery and taking photos of fast food restaurant signs.

Eric wrote many of the subdivision regulations and the road construction ordinances. Some of the other ordinances, including the zoning plan, were adopted directly from Knoxville or Knox County. Sometimes that was done to save time or to adopt something quickly that could be edited later. Other times it was to avoid lawsuits or other problems.

On anything controversial—usually anything that changed current regulations too much, or that would offend long-time landowners—the vote was almost always three to two. Marianne, Eric and George were never sure if Eddy and Bob were just much more conservative than they were, or if the incorporation battle lines were being drawn all over again.

In any case, the votes were often predictable, even if the situation was not.

But after the initial discussions and arguments and the obligatory 3-to-2 vote, the second reading of each ordinance went much quicker.

Each Board member would pick a section of each ordinance and read them aloud simultaneously. It was cacophonous and impossible to understand, but it was quick.

Ford, especially, despised this process, later saying it made him feel stupid to have everything read aloud at once. But the sheer volume of ordinances and rules Farragut's first Board had to create, write, read aloud and approve was not the only thing that made the meetings long. There was no shortage of controversy at the meetings—both among Board members and from residents of the community. McGill and Leonard, especially, butted heads in arguments that frequently warranted mention in the newspapers.

Developers and realtors also often made appearances before the Board, most trying to get a handle on just how to deal with Farragut's new ordinances.

And that wasn't an unusual position—most everyone was still trying to get a good grasp on the new town and just what it meant.

The Fallout

Fall 1980

Ralph and Marianne groaned when they looked out the window that morning.

Yards upon yards of toilet paper had been strung across their yard, over the tree limbs and bushes, thrown over the roof and between the porch rails, over their cars and mailboxes. And confetti was everywhere. Simply … everywhere. It was by far the largest TP job either of them had ever seen.

It certainly wasn't a violent crime and it wasn't even that damaging. A harmless prank is what some would consider it.

And, no doubt, it was the work of a couple of teenagers.

But it wasn't because of a childish high school argument or some lost competition—it was because of the incorporation. And it was because Marianne was serving on the Board, that group that was passing prohibitive sign ordinances and restrictive controls on development and drainage. Marianne set down her coffee, too frustrated to eat breakfast. She grabbed a trash bag and a rake and set out to clean up the mess. The damp grass made the toilet paper rip and bunch on the grass.

It was going to take a long time to clean.

"You just know that these kids have heard their parents complaining about us," Marianne told Ralph as he joined her.

"I bet I could even guess whose kids did this," she groused.

And that was true.

The toilet paper was certainly not the most threatening thing that happened to Board members, or that had happened to the McGills. Marianne and Ralph still remembered the night Ralph was tailed home by an incorporation opponent.

The incorporation had been successful, but the anger and frustration in the community was still there.

And maybe it was some of those same people—the ones who had so violently opposed incorporation—that were responsible for the current form of harassment, maybe even the toilet paper. At least indirectly, since it was most likely their teenaged children who had acted out on the frustration.

Marianne gritted her teeth as the phone continued to ring.

The frustration was still there, still manifesting in harassment, but the type of harassment had changed. There'd not been another attempted run-over in a parking lot. Now it was phone calls: calls in the middle of the night, sometimes to make a legitimate complaint, but most designed just to wake each elected official up, just to frighten them.

After the Board meeting a few weeks ago, Marianne had received a phone call at two in the morning. The sound had startled her out of her sleep, but it didn't surprise her. It had become a routine. Someone called after nearly every single meeting.

Most of the time, Marianne would say, "Hello?" but no one would answer. All she could hear was breathing into the phone. The first few times, she had asked who was calling repeatedly, increasingly frustrated and frightened. But soon after that, Marianne realized she was not the only Board member getting calls.

And none of them had any trouble guessing who was calling.

"I know it's you!" Marianne had called out, more than once, into the receiver.

The man, the one Eric called Liberty Valance, was considered by the Group members to be a drunk and it was well known that he was so opposed to the Town he was considering suing or even paying for a re-vote referendum. He owned a store on the far western side of Town and had posted signs barring Farragut officials from entering it. Not that they would want to.

He would keep up the calling for years.

After Betty Dick was elected to the Board in 1981, the man would call her in the middle of the night. Jeremy would answer the phone, listen to the silence for a few moments, and then hand it over, groaning, "It's for you."

As far as anyone knew, it was only members of the Farragut Community Group who received the calls. Ford would later deny he'd ever received any. The calls disturbed Ron Simandl so much that he called the FBI and, during one or two contentious voting issues, considered sending his wife and son to stay with family in Florida. In fact, he was so unnerved that the years he served on the Board after taking Eric Johnson's seat were his only foray into elected office.

Jan Johnson ironed her clothes with a pistol in the chair beside her. Jan also eventually purchased recording equipment and taped every call she received from the man. After a second TP incident, Ralph bought a gun.

But that wasn't when the harassers crossed the line.

That happened when Jan and Eric's children said their bus had been followed one Friday when they were coming home from school. The couple could handle the phone calls. What they could not handle was when someone trailed his children.

Jan called the police immediately, and they drove through the subdivision for two weeks after the incident, on the watch for any suspicious vehicles. And after the Board meeting that week, Eric sat by the phone, waiting for the call he knew was coming. When it did, Eric made one promise: "I know it's you. And you should know that I hunt and I target shoot, and if you get close, I won't miss."

That didn't stop the calls or the anger, but there were never any more tailing incidents. Nor did Valance ever allow Farragut officials or staff into his business.

Marianne snapped out of her reverie when someone answered the phone. She quickly explained the situation, listened for a bit and then hung up the receiver. She smiled to herself and walked across the house to her front room, settling into a chair by the window, where she could watch the teenagers down the street clean up the mess in her yard.

The Staff

October 1980

Mary Lou Koepp peered into the drawer of the filing cabinet and pulled out a one-inch folder.

She raised an eyebrow. "So this is an ordinance?" she thought. She'd never worked for a government. She'd had no idea what an ordinance was when she accepted the job as town recorder, but she was too embarrassed to ask anyone. Millie McBride had just gone home after showing Koepp around the office and taking her to the post office to pick up the mail. Mary Lou put the file back in the drawer then sat in the chair at the wooden desk in the large back room behind the savings and loan.

The chair, desk and two four-drawer filing cabinets were the only furniture in the room. On the desk sat a phone and a Selectric typewriter; nearby was a rented copier.

Mary Lou and her husband, Tom, lived in Village Green, four doors down from the McGills. She'd been a teacher for years and recently had been working for The University of Tennessee as a receptionist.

When McBride had told her at the Village Green Independence Day picnic that she had no plans to take the town recorder position permanently, Mary Lou sent in her résumé.

"They're looking for someone who can type sixty words a minute and write shorthand at eighty words a minute!" McBride had told her. That just happened to be Mary Lou's specialty. Shorthand and typing were what she'd taught for years.

But Mary Lou didn't hear back from anyone about her resume for more than two months. Finally, Farragut hiring committee members contacted her to set up an interview with the committee on a Saturday morning.

"I'm not sure I'll go," she told her husband Tom. "There's a football game Saturday afternoon."

She did go after all and was interviewed by a committee that included Eddy Ford's wife, Linda, and Bob Leonard. Then she went to the football game and tried to get over her nerves. Leonard contacted her early the next week and offered her the job, which she took after working out her two weeks' notice for William Snyder, who'd later become a UT chancellor and retire to be organist at the Tennessee Theater.

In that first week of work, Mary Lou received a check for $15,000 for beer permit money. It was the most money she'd ever seen at one time. She called Millie excitedly. "I just got a check for $15,000!" she told Millie. "What am I supposed to do with it?"

"Well. I would take it to the bank to deposit it," Millie said matter-of-factly.

Mary Lou stayed busy, attending the Board of Mayor and Aldermen meetings every Thursday, typing up ordinances—now she knew what they were—and dealing with occasional phone calls and visitors. Not that there were many, especially in those first few months.

By late winter 1981, Farragut had enough money in its coffers to hire a town administrator, its second employee after town recorder Koepp.

A group of citizens, acting as a personnel committee, whittled down dozens of resumes to the final two, then the candidates had individual interviews with each member of Farragut's Board of Mayor and Aldermen. The position went to Jack Hamlett. Hamlett, a native of East Tennessee, was impressed with the vision of the start-up community, so he, his wife and two small sons left a home in South Carolina, moved to Farragut in February and stayed for fourteen years.

He led the elected officials of Farragut into cutting-edge practices at the time, including contracting out for services, something rarely done by municipalities in the '80s. He helped draft the zoning ordinance, zoning map, land use plan and comprehensive zoning plan; helped write or edit almost every ordinance that regulated the streets of Farragut. He hired the early staff, literally deciding on the faces and personalities that would help shape the Town.

Hamlett made a point of hiring disparate personalities from diverse backgrounds, believing the mix of those with institutional history— like Mary Lou, who lived in Village Green—and those like himself, who could bring ideas from other parts of the country, made for a beneficial mix. And over time, Hamlett built the staff up, hiring codes enforcers, an engineer and public works crews.

"There's no 'This is the way it's always been done' here," he would say.

But for the first few years, Koepp and Hamlett were the only full-time employees, doing a bit of everything, pitching in to help Bill Maney, the retired engineer from TDOT that reffed football games with Eddy Ford and who stood in occasionally as a sometime engineer and public works director.

Farragut's offices remained in the back office behind the savings and loan for five years, then moved to an old dairy farm building behind the historic Campbell Inn—for which Campbell's Station was named—before moving into an actual Town Hall.

Ron Simandl

Ron Simandl remembers the incorporation effort as a snowball.

He'd been carpooling with Eric Johnson and Dewey Young. That had led to attending county commission and planning commission meetings. That had led to incorporation discussions. That led to putting together a town. And finally, that resulted in Simandl running for alderman.

Simandl took office in 1981, moving into Eric Johnson's seat.

"That snowball just got bigger and bigger," Simandl laughs, sitting at his kitchen table, just a few streets away from the McGills' later Farragut home in Sugarwood.

Simandl isn't a politician. He's a chemist. By his own admittance, he never intended to be an elected official, and had no interest in doing it more than once. It was too stressful. Particularly the harassment.

"I couldn't take the late night phone calls. It got to me," he says.

One-on-one, he tells a chronological, historical recounting of his time with the Farragut Community Group and his years as an alderman. Unlike many of the other Group members, Simandl is remarkably impartial. He tends to remember events very logically, even clinically, throwing in his opinions or personal comments as a side-note, a caboose to the train of the main story.

And to Simandl, the main story is the underdog tale of how a small group of homeowners charged down a city trying to take control of them … and how they won.

"It's David and Goliath. We were going to change the world, right?" Simandl says, grinning.

Simandl's humor is dry, subtle. His square jaw doesn't alter much when he smiles, but his eyes give him away. The rest of the Farragut Community Group remembers Simandl as the near-constant companion to Eric Johnson's endless jokes. And the pair's birthdays are only three days apart, making them the youngest members of the Group. Simandl does tell jokes, but his are a bit slyer than Johnson's outright laugh-out-loud turns of phrase. But it's easy to see how Simandl's dry humor would be the perfect catalyst to some of Johnson's jokes.

He sings a line of the song "You Don't Mess Around with Jim," when remembering David Rodgers: "You don't tug on superman's cape."

Simandl tends to remember everyone else's contributions to the incorporation effort and their time on the Board of Mayor and Aldermen more than his own. But Simandl served on the Board when the Town decided to fix the seventeen percent grade on Peterson Road, changing it to allow for better sight distance.

It was during that process that the Board was accused of breaking the Sunshine Law, which states elected officials must vote in public meetings, and can't discuss votes outside those meetings. Members of that first Board met out on Peterson one afternoon to discuss the road and the re-grading that would be necessary to fix it, including cutting into peoples' yards and repaving the entire thing. If you ask the Board members, they remember press representatives being there, and also remember not discussing amongst themselves, only asking questions.

In any case, the Sunshine Law violation allegations never amounted to much.

Not that the allegations were the only controversy Simandl

encountered during his time on the Board. A particularly long-lived lawsuit with a local landowner and developer dragged on, as did various suits from the city and the county.

"And we still had tons of ordinances to pass," Simandl says, leaning back in his chair, remembering the lengthy nights of reading ordinances aloud, one at a time.

By 1981, the Town had established both the Board and its Planning Commission, and was busily writing new ordinances and rewriting county ordinances that had been adopted as a stopgap. That's not to say that none of them were adopted without controversy, or even disagreement among Board members. But Simandl doesn't remember the Board as being dissonant, necessarily.

"None of the disagreements were personal," he says. There were harsh words at times, but in the end, everyone had to compromise a little and the results were generally accepted by all.

Simandl has especially glowing words for Ford and Leonard, calling them "neutral ground" that residents who hadn't necessarily advocated incorporation could get behind. And Simandl, who stepped down from elected office in 1983, has been watching the growth of the Town—without much partiality, even for his extensive work with Farragut Community Group—for a long time.

When he's remembering his time with the Farragut Community Group and as an alderman, Simandl seems a bit incredulous that any of it happened, or perhaps, that he was involved with any of it as deeply as he was.

The most concrete evidence of the town's success, he says, is that Farragut simply looks different than other parts of the city and county. Not in a superior way, but in a way that makes you proud to live there. And that was Simandl's goal all along.

"If you're going to live somewhere, you want it to look nice," he says.

The Blackmail

September 1980

The charges were first printed in a *News-Sentinel* article by Jan Maxwell-Avent, headlined "Farragut Developer Charges Blackmail."

Keith McCord, the attorney for Moser-Biddle Corporation, accused Farragut's Board—and specifically Marianne McGill—of harassment and blackmail. Moser-Biddle had plans to build a Wendy's fast food restaurant along Kingston Pike, along with a K-Mart, but faced a number of obstacles soon after the Town was incorporated, most revolving around the fact Moser-Biddle had received approval from the county for the project before the town existed.

Once Farragut incorporated, the Board clearly believed it should have to approve the plans as well.

That was an idea McCord and the developer, Culan Biddle, did not agree with.

In a prepared statement dated September 25, 1980, McCord laid out his accusations, accented with capital letters and underlined words for emphasis.

Culan Biddle and his wife owned around 250 acres of land on the far east side of Farragut, close to the schools. The land had been passed down by Biddle's father-in-law, J.G. Moser. Biddle had submitted a development plan for his property in 1978 to the county's metropolitan planning commission—a plan that included commercial areas fronting Kingston Pike and residential areas behind that. The county approved it.

By 1980, when the Town was formed, only one phase of the four-phase development had been built. Plans for K-Mart, in the second phase of the development, were approved by the county January 14, 1980—one day before Farragut incorporated.

In March, when Biddle got around to applying for a rezoning to commercial use for the land, the county commission refused to vote, saying that responsibility now lay with the newly formed Farragut. Biddle was, however, given a building permit for the K-Mart—and for a fast food restaurant designated as a Burger King at the time—over the next few weeks. In July, at the behest of a financier, Biddle submitted the plans to Farragut.

He considered it a courtesy.

Farragut's Board considered it out of line.

"At the request of our lender, we agreed to present the plans to the Town of Farragut without any legal obligation to do so and without any right on the part of the Town to have the plans reviewed or presented … because the Town of Farragut had adopted no ordinances requiring a building permit," McCord's statement said.

Although the plans met existing ordinance regulations—Knox County's—Farragut's newly formed municipal planning commission and Board delayed action on the plans.

"The attitude reflected by you was indeed shocking," McCord stated.

"When we told you of the risk of financial loss that we would suffer as a result of any delay, one of your members responded, 'That's not our problem.' We suggested to you that a delay could result in the loss of the K-Mart project and one of your members responded, 'That's all right, we don't need it.'"

The day after the meeting at which those comments were uttered, July 18, newspapers declared the Board had proposed ordinances establishing building permits, establishing a building code and resisting extensive curb cuts.

"Some of these ordinances were not even typed, but were put together with glue and tape, consisting of hand written paragraphs and typed paragraphs. Your intent is obvious ... to adopt these ordinances on second reading and therefore attempt to have them apply to the K-Mart project," McCord's statement said.

In response, Biddle began construction on the project immediately, July 21.

The Town, in return, told Biddle and McCord that while the K-Mart might not need a building permit from the Town at the moment, it would need a certificate of occupancy.

And the Town would not issue one.

"Not only did you make this threat to us, but you conveyed it to the K-Mart Corporation. The fact and truth of the matter is at the time that threat was made, you had no ordinance calling for a certificate of occupancy and you knew it," McCord's statement read, underlines and all.

He alleged Farragut's incorporators had an express purpose of preventing "any commercial development within the Town." He also alleged a particular member of Farragut's Board told Biddle "there would be no K mart and no fast food restaurant constructed on the property." In later conversations, it came out that Biddle and McCord accused Marianne McGill of making that comment, which the pair considered rather egregious.

For her part, Marianne denied saying it. She later would say she suspected she had been confused with Jan Johnson, who also was petite and dark-haired.

After the Town's declaration that it would not grant any certificate of occupancy, McCord alleged the Board was advised by David Rodgers, and secondarily by Bob Leonard, that the Board was acting improperly by threatening to withhold a certificate of occupancy. The pair of attorneys warned that a refusal to grant a certificate of occupancy could threaten the development: the tenants could pull out of the project, as could the financiers. Rodgers and Leonard advised the Board approve a "no action letter," negating their threat, at a meeting July 22.

The Board didn't approve it.

"You had a responsibility, duty and obligation to correct the wrong that you had set in motion and you abrogated that responsibility in a rather arrogant manner," McCord said in his letter.

As a result, Moser-Biddle claimed it lost $300,000 in a bond sale that was cancelled.

"You finally did approve a 'no action letter' after extracting from the M-B Corp. certain commitments and agreements which were totally beyond the realm of responsible governmental action. You are now calling that letter and agreement a cooperative venture," McCord went on.

"My clients call it BLACKMAIL, because you used the power of office without supporting law to force upon a citizen of this community concession that you knew could not otherwise be obtained."

McCord then laid out plans for the remaining 150 acres of Biddle's property, which was largely being used as a horse field in 1980. About the effect of his letter, he said, "the air is cleared."

"I would hope that you are willing to clear the air as we have attempted to do."

Biddle and McCord didn't let the matter drop.

By June 1981, they sued the Board for $1.9 million, and Tennessee Municipal League—the Town's insurer—ultimately paid to defend the suit. The Biddle lawsuit languished in courts for years, not really pushed forward further by either party. Rodgers mostly let it be.

"You never kick a sleeping dog," he would say.

The Biddle property remained largely a horse field at the time of the town's thirtieth anniversary in 2010, with plans still in place to develop the property in phases. The first phase of the Brooklawn development, as it is called, included a Kroger Marketplace, the first built east of the Mississippi.

The Wendy's and K-Mart, which eventually were built on the property, had by then been replaced by other tenants.

David Rodgers

Ask any of the founders of Farragut, and they will tell you Farragut would be nonexistent without David Rodgers. They'll tell you David took a dream, a fantasy, and turned it into reality with little more than a wide determined streak and a way with words. They'll make it clear Rodgers filled in the gaps they couldn't. They'll be the first to tell you David had something everyone else just ... didn't.

And that might be true. It's certain he had gumption, determination, vision. But many of the founders had those things. Factually, he did have one thing no other founder had.

Age.

He was forty-five when Betty Dick phoned him about the incorporation idea, forty-six when he was named Town attorney. Thrown in with a bunch of thirty-somethings, Rodgers had more life experience than many of them. He knew more about what they were getting into, the responsibilities they'd face. But he was never one to back down from a fight.

"You have not practiced law until you've incorporated your own town from scratch," he would tell the *Knoxville Journal* in 1990. "You don't have any ordinances. You don't have a staff. You don't have a paper clip."

"All you have is a gleam in your eye."

David's wife, Marty, remembers "He initially felt it would be overwhelming, but it only took one meeting for him to decide to go out 'guns a-blazin'.'"

David Rodgers passed away in 2010.

David met Marty in Nashville, while he was at law school at Vanderbilt and she was at Peabody College. He remained a lifelong Vandy fan, even after moving to University of Tennessee-obsessed Knoxville. He joked he was a "split personality," supporting both teams. Rodgers was born in Nashville, one of the few incorporators that hailed from the south; and grew up not far from Knoxville, in a small town called La Follette.

Perhaps it was that small-town, Southern upbringing that gave Rodgers many of his folksy sayings, words he'd use with friends and in courtrooms, peculiar turns of phrase he'd be remembered for even after his death.

He called his closest friends "pardnah," a term Ralph McGill memorialized thirty years after the incorporation on a plaque placed in Farragut's town hall in David's honor, purchased by members of Farragut Community Group. His personal motto, as quoted in newspaper profile articles, was the Golden Rule: "Do unto others as you would have them do unto you." Well-known phrases like "You never kick a sleeping dog" and "You catch more flies with honey than with vinegar" made their way into David's lexicon, often referring to clients, dueling attorneys and even judges.

"When he talked, you listened," says Marty, sitting in the front sitting room of the Village Green home she and David shared, frequently glancing toward the chair across the room, his chair.

She remembers one of the couple's four sons saying speaking to his father was like taking a verbal SAT test. But she also remembers David's humor—often sly and dry, always witty.

On that count, Tom Hale, David's apprentice and Farragut's second attorney, remembers David saying, "'Pigs get fat, but hogs get slaughtered.' In other words, it's OK to be piggish but not OK to be hoggish," Hale says. "Clients loved that one."

By all accounts, Rodgers was a masterful municipal attorney— admired and befriended even by his opponents in the courtroom, including fellow attorneys Jon Roach and Randy Tyree. In fact, his prowess gave credence to his firm, Kramer Rayson, in terms of municipal law. According to Hale, David never made any argument he didn't believe, reasoning powerful arguments could be made only about beliefs you strongly hold.

"He would research a topic, check everything was accurate and then construct persuasive arguments," says Hale, rifling through notes and lawsuits David had his hand in, frequently referring to a eulogy he wrote for his mentor.

For David, there was no preparing multiple arguments for a case, no arguing every possible reasoning before a judge. Rodgers didn't like to waste time, so he picked the best argument and argued it to within an inch of its life.

"And that's why he always won," Hale says.

Jack Hamlett saw the same thing.

Rodgers would look at a legal matter and give his strict, by-the-book legal opinion, what Hamlett said David called his "belt and suspenders opinion." Then he'd turn around and tell you the commonsense way to handle it.

Common sense seems to be the prevailing term when it comes to describing David Rodgers. It's the term most used to talk about his personality, his practice and his stance on the Town's legal matters. The second-most used word to describe Rodgers is, without a doubt, "gentlemanly."

He considered the city of Knoxville's Interstate annexation

ridiculous, and made no bones about that in newspaper article after article. Hearing David described, it's easy to see that his deep objection wasn't because such an annexation endangered Farragut. It was because it didn't make sense.

"Those were kind of 'iffy' things, and David was not an 'iffy' guy. That was not a lucid thought to him, even," Marty says.

Largely through his work with the Town, Rodgers became one of the most respected municipal attorneys in the state.

But Marty said he never cared much about accolades or recognition. He was in it because he cared.

"He was totally invested in the Town. He wanted to be on the Farragut team to fight," she says. That's why he helped the Farragut Community Group, spending late nights coming up with incorporation plans. And that's why he agreed to become Farragut's attorney, which meant more late nights, more legal work and more lawsuits.

According to Marty, David never considered running for office, an idea bandied about in many of the papers during the 1980 elections. The courtroom was his area of expertise. And that's where he would stay.

"That was what he could do well, and other people could do well on the Board of Mayor and Aldermen," Marty says.

Rodgers would always consider his work with the Town the greatest professional work of his life.

"I used to go boating and play some tennis, but now it seems that my hobbies have simply been the town of Farragut," he joked with a *Sentinel* reporter in 1981.

"I am as proud of the work I have done for Farragut as anything I've ever done in my professional career," he told *Journal* reporter Angie Gardner in 1989.

"I feel almost about the town like I do my children. You take on one of them, and you've got a fight," Suzanne Foree Neal quoted him as saying in a 1990 article in the *News-Sentinel*.

April Fool's Day

April 1, 1981

It garnered a call from Washington D.C.

The April Fool's joke had been dreamed up by Eric. No surprise there: the youngest member of the former Farragut Community Group was forever annoying Bob Leonard and Eddy Ford with his jokes. But this was one joke Leonard refused to even recognize.

Near the end of the meeting, when Leonard asked if any of the Board members had additional business, Eric passed out a simple map he'd drawn of Knoxville's borders. Around the entire border, he had drawn a pencil line. There was a state law, which Knoxville used to do its finger annexations, that would allow one city to annex land surrounding another city with just a simple ordinance, so long as it was within a certain maximum area. Eric had spent several nights calculating the exact number that could be allowed under the law, and was now presenting it to the Board.

Eric had considered the joke to be a funny way of turning the tables on the city that had caused them so much stress during the incorporation effort. After the last year of long meetings and arguments over nearly every single zoning and building code and aesthetic standard, it would be nice to sit in a meeting and laugh.

"This is an ordinance to annex certain territory and to incorporate same within the corporate boundaries of the town of Farragut, Tennessee," Eric told the other board members.

David winked at Eric, then read out the ordinance Eric had written up:

WHEREAS, the prosperity of this town may be materially retarded and the safety and welfare of its inhabitants and property thereof endangered if such territory is not annexed. WHEREAS the State Supreme Court, in all its wisdom, has determined interstate annexation to be necessary for the safety and welfare of Knoxville; and WHEREAS, that vulture which has gobbled up an interstate highway and the centerline of Kingston Pike may still be hungry; NOW, THEREFORE, be it ordained by the Town of Farragut, Tennessee: Section 1. Pursuant to authority conferred by sections 6-308 to 6-320 Tennessee Code Annotated, there is hereby annexed to the Town of Farragut, Tennessee, the following described territory: Start at the centerline of the intersection of I-40 and Campbell Station Road, head in a clockwise direction using a radius of 9.84 miles and a width of one foot with the center point of being the intersection of Lyons View Drive and Kingston Pike and continue a 360-degree circle back to the starting point. Total area equals 74.9 acres. (See attached map.) This annexation will completely encircle Knoxville and prevent any future annexation of adjacent highways, therefore protecting Knox County, East Tennessee, and possibly Middle Tennessee from future Knoxville annexations. Section 2. This ordinance shall be considered at 12:01 a.m., April Fool's Day, 1981.

Down the dais, David, who had been in on the joke from the beginning, bowed his head to hide his chuckle. George, who had helped

Eric put finishing touches on the ordinance, and Marianne, choked on their own laughter, tears running down their cheeks.

But Bob didn't see the humor.

"We'll have none of this!" he exclaimed. "I want no surprises at our meetings!"

Eric moved to adopt that ordinance and George seconded. But there was too much laughter to get around to taking a vote.

The next day, a Knoxville paper printed a story about the meeting as if the ordinance had actually passed, although, of course, Johnson had never meant it to go to a vote in any case.

But the news traveled quickly—even nationwide—and soon, Johnson was answering the phone to a call from a congressman's office in Washington D.C., where the news had earned a mention in the *Washington Post*.

"Is that actually legal? We have a similar problem up here," Johnson remembers the man on the other line asking him.

"Well, it'd be legal. But look at the date, friend. Look at the date," Johnson told him. He, as usual, got the last laugh.

Epilogue

In 2012, Farragut still operates without a property tax and is well known for its strict aesthetic building standards and adherence to proper zoning and building codes. Farragut provides its citizens with parks, roads and community events, and places great importance on volunteers for everything from manning the Farragut Folklife Museum to sitting on the Municipal Planning Commission. Knox County operates the school system, library system and provides police protection. Farragut residents subscribe to another entity for fire protection.

Bob Leonard served as Farragut's mayor for thirteen years. Eddy Ford succeeded him in 1993, and was mayor for sixteen years.

Most members of the Farragut Community Group, as well as early volunteers and even employees, still reside in Farragut, and several are still active on Farragut citizen committees. Betty Dick serves on Farragut's Municipal Planning Commission, and she and Jeremy have four grandchildren. Eric Johnson is retired and spends time with his five grandchildren, golfing and reading history books. Bill and Karen Etter retired and moved to Dandridge in 2004, after Bill served 10 years as commissioner for First Utility District, becoming friends with Bob Leonard through the same company he'd criticized during the incorporation effort. Gene McNalley enjoys spending time with his children and grandchildren and "fussing" about Congress. George and Julie Dorsey both retired from Lockheed Martin Energy Systems in

Oak Ridge, and enjoy traveling, spending time with grandchildren and playing golf.

Ralph and Marianne McGill watched Farragut from the sidelines after Marianne left the Board of Mayor and Aldermen in 1984, until Ralph ran and was elected mayor in 2009. His term ends in August 2014. They have four granddaughters and enjoy traveling and their church. Ralph is "semi-retired," consulting occasionally for the International Energy Agency.

Ron Simandl, as of the time of the writing of this book, was still working at the Department of Energy facilities in Oak Ridge, TN.

Jess Campbell and David Rodgers passed away in 2010. Bob Leonard died in 2012.

~

"When the legend becomes fact, print the legend."
— The Man Who Shot Liberty Valance